THE UNEXPECTED EXODUS

SOUTHERN CLASSICS SERIES
John G. Sproat and Mark M. Smith, Series Editors

THE UNEXPECTED EXODUS

How the Cold War Displaced One Southern Town

LOUISE CASSELS

New Introduction by Kari Frederickson

The University of South Carolina Press

Published in Cooperation with the Institute for
Southern Studies of the University of South Carolina

© 1971 Louise Cassels
New material © 2007 University of South Carolina

Cloth edition published by Sand Hill Press, 1971
Paperback edition published by the University of South Carolina Press,
Columbia, South Carolina 29208

www.sc.edu/uscpress

Manufactured in the United States of America

16 15 14 13 12 11 10 09 08 07   10 9 8 7 6 5 4 3 2 1

Library of Congress Cataloging-in-Publication Data

Cassels, Louise.
  The unexpected exodus : how the Cold War displaced one southern town / Louise
Cassels ; new Introduction by Kari Frederickson.
    p. cm. — (Southern classics series)
  "Published in cooperation with the Institute for Southern Studies of the University of
South Carolina."
  Originally published: Aiken, S.C. : Sand Hill Press, 1971.
  Includes bibliographical references.
  ISBN-13: 978-1-57003-709-2 (pbk : alk. paper)
  ISBN-10: 1-57003-709-4 (pbk : alk. paper)
  1. Cassels, Louise. 2. Ellenton (S.C.)—Biography. 3. Ellenton (S.C.)—History—
20th century. 4. Cold War—Social aspects—South Carolina—Ellenton. 5. Savannah
River Plant (E.I. du Pont de Nemours & Company)—History. 6. U.S. Atomic Energy
Commission. Savannah River Operations Office—History. 7. Nuclear weapons
plants—Social aspects—South Carolina—Ellenton—History—20th century.
8. Ellenton (S.C.)—Social life and customs—20th century. 9. Ellenton (S.C.)—
Social conditions—20th century. I. University of South Carolina. Institute for
Southern Studies. II. Title.
  F279.E42C37 2007
  975.7'75043092—dc22
  [B]

                                                                    2007022334

Publication of the Southern Classics series is made possible in part by the generous
support of the Watson-Brown Foundation.

CONTENTS

ILLUSTRATIONS

SERIES EDITORS' PREFACE

As Kari Frederickson's helpful new introduction to Louise Cassels's *The Unexpected Exodus* explains, the cold war impacted the post–World War II South in interesting and revealing ways. Cassels grants readers tremendous and unusually detailed access to the demographic, social, economic, and political effects of the militarization and modernization of the southern economy by describing the forced relocation of eight thousand South Carolinians to make way for the Savannah River Plant in 1952. Cassels tells the story of Ellenton, the largest of the communities affected, charting the effect of the evacuation on her family and community. Told with style and passion, *The Unexpected Exodus* is more than memoir. It is a story of the South's modernization, one detailing how a southern sense of place encountered postwar international realties, and a powerful reminder about how ideas of sacrifice, national security, individual liberty, and property rights and responsibilities increasingly became the stuff of postwar southern discourse and experience.

Southern Classics returns to general circulation books of importance dealing with the history and culture of the American South. Sponsored by the Institute for Southern Studies, the series is advised by a board of distinguished scholars who suggest titles and editors of individual volumes to the series editors and help establish priorities in publication.

Chronological age alone does not determine a title's designation as a Southern Classic. The criteria also include significance in contributing to a broad understanding of the region, timeliness in relation to events and moments of peculiar interest to the American South, usefulness in the classroom, and suitability for inclusion in personal and institutional collections on the region.

Mark M. Smith
John G. Sproat
Series Editors

NEW INTRODUCTION

On September 3, 1949, a United States Air Force WB-29 flying east of the Kamchatka Peninsula in the Soviet Union on a routine (but secret) detection flight picked up radioactivity in its filters. Measurements of the filter paper confirmed that the radioactivity was man-made. American scientists tracked the radioactive air mass for the next two weeks as it drifted across the Pacific Ocean and then across the United States.

Tracerlab at the University of California at Berkeley estimated that the radioactivity came from a device of Soviet origin and that the explosion had taken place on August 29, 1949. On the morning of September 23, 1949, armed with scientific data from American and British experts, a somber President Harry Truman informed the nation that the Soviets had exploded an atomic bomb. After four short years America's nuclear monopoly was ended. The world had become a much more dangerous place.

The discovery that the Soviet Union possessed nuclear capabilities escalated discussions at the nation's highest levels over whether the United States should proceed with production of the hydrogen bomb, a thermonuclear device whose destructive capabilities were projected to be one hundred times greater than those of existing atomic weapons. Senator Brien McMahon, a Democrat from Connecticut and chair of the Joint Congressional Committee on Atomic Energy, pressured the president. "If we let Russia get the Super first, catastrophe becomes all but certain," he warned, "whereas if we get it first, there exists a chance of saving ourselves." On January 31, 1950, Truman authorized an accelerated program to develop the hydrogen bomb.[1]

The intense discussions over the production of the hydrogen bomb—and the broader question of the role of atomic weapons in the nation's military and foreign policy—were spurred by developments at home and around the globe. In October 1949, shortly after the discovery that the Soviets had the bomb, Communist forces consolidated their control over mainland China, escalating fears of a Moscow-Beijing Communist alliance against the Western democracies. The trial of Alger Hiss in late 1949 and his conviction for perjury in January 1950—quickly followed by the discovery of an espionage ring at Los Alamos—ignited fears of internal threats to national security. New realities dictated new policy, and in the spring of 1950 the president directed the State Department's policy-planning staff to review the nation's security needs. The result was National Security Council Document #68 (NSC-68). Among other recommendations, NSC-68 proposed meeting the growing Soviet threat with a large arsenal of nuclear weapons.[2] A new plant to create material for the world's first thermonuclear weapon would constitute a key component of this beefed-up arsenal.

To build this new plant, the Atomic Energy Commission (AEC) contracted with the Du Pont Corporation of Delaware. A leader in weapons production, Du Pont had constructed and operated the world's first plutonium-production reactors at Hanford, Washington, as part of the Manhattan Project.[3] In mid-1950 AEC and Du Pont officials crisscrossed the country, investigating 114 potential production sites.[4] The ideal location they sought would combine "low population density, proximity to a fairly large urban center, a local labor supply, and an adequate supply of water of specified purity."[5] Their assignment acquired heightened urgency when—in the early hours of Sunday, June 25, 1950—thousands of North Koreans poured southward over the 38th parallel. The Korean War had begun. Five months later, on November 28, 1950—only a few days after Chinese troops crossed the Yalu River, threatening to turn the Korean conflict into a larger Asian land war—the AEC announced that it had chosen a site on the western edge of South Carolina, bordering the Savannah River.[6] A massive undertaking, the plant, ultimately known as the Savannah River Plant, would rest on more than two hundred thousand acres of land in Aiken, Barnwell, and Allendale counties.[7]

Although a complex combination of environmental, construction, safety, and population factors determined the location of the plant, good old-fashioned politicking and planning also played a part. The

Savannah River Plant was just the latest in a string of federal projects that South Carolina lawmakers had courted. In 1935, thanks to aggressive lobbying by state leaders, President Franklin Roosevelt had approved the Santee Cooper hydroelectric and flood-control project, which became one of the largest New Deal undertakings in the nation. The Clarks Hill Project, one dam in what eventually became a series of eleven dams along the Savannah River, was approved by the Flood Control Act of 1944 and completed in 1954.[8] State senator Edgar Brown of Barnwell, South Carolina, nicknamed the Bishop of Barnwell and Mr. Big, was instrumental in securing the Clarks Hill Project, viewing it as a critical first step in regional development. The Clarks Hill Project improved river navigation, promoted flood control, and provided power and recreation to the region. When approached by the AEC about Barnwell County as a possible location for the hydrogen-bomb plant, Brown "linked the completion of the federal dam project to the new Savannah River Plant." The South Carolina Research, Planning, and Development Board supplemented Brown's efforts by marshaling pertinent data on Aiken and Barnwell counties in promotional brochures. The completion of the Clarks Hill dam and its ability to provide hydroelectric power to the region helped to secure the Savannah River Plant for South Carolina. According to one historian of the site, "the presence of the smaller fish had enticed a larger fish into the pond."[9] Construction began on February 1, 1951, and operations at the plant commenced on October 3, 1952.[10] The plant cost more than $2 billion to build and was the largest construction project to date in the United States, on a par with the building of the Panama Canal. One reporter noted that "the dirt excavated would build a barrier as large as the Great Wall of China from coast to coast."[11]

The Savannah River Plant—what locals would call "the bomb plant"—was just one of scores of cold-war projects that changed the face of the South. The militarization of the southern economy began during World War II, when new shipbuilding, aircraft, and munitions plants dotted the southern landscape. To a region hit especially hard by the Great Depression, the wartime boom was an economic godsend. Nevertheless, although the impact of wartime federal projects in the

South was impressive and unprecedented, the South did not receive its share of federal spending in comparison with other regions. But as hot war turned to cold, the southern states more than made up for this disparity. Private industries competed for lucrative defense contracts; states aggressively pursued funds for highway and airport construction; and the fledgling space program created new avenues of research and development that transformed sleepy southern towns in northern Alabama and along the east coast of Florida into high-tech outposts. In terms of its dependence on the defense establishment for both employment and income, the South surpassed the national average.[12]

Cold-war industries brought thousands of newcomers to the South, where they settled in the region's burgeoning suburbs. Almost overnight, areas of the South in which the majority of adults had not graduated from high school suddenly found themselves awash in Ph.D.'s. Accompanying the newcomers were new churches, universities, shopping malls, and other trappings of a more cosmopolitan lifestyle. In addition to attracting new residents, these high-tech cold-war installations also provided opportunities for long-term residents, who before could look forward only to a lifetime of toil in the region's low-wage industries.

The onset of the cold war, the militarization of the southern economy, and the modernization of the region came with huge costs. To make way for the Savannah River Plant, some fifteen hundred families (approximately eight thousand individuals) living within the plant's boundaries had to be evacuated.[13] Families who had lived in the region for generations had to start over somewhere else. There were several small communities within the plant's proposed borders. The largest of these towns was Ellenton, population 760.

The Unexpected Exodus is Louise Cassels's memoir of her forced evacuation from her hometown of Ellenton, South Carolina, in 1952. The daughter of one of Ellenton's most entrepreneurial families, Cassels was a schoolteacher by training and an astute observer by nature. With clarity and honesty this book provides a unique look at the local and personal impact of the expanding and menacing cold war. Throughout her brief tale, Cassels's emotions run the gamut from proud and patriotic to resentful and melancholy, as she and her neighbors try to comprehend the fate that has befallen them and the great sacrifice they must make. Cassels's story is a poignant testimony to the power of place and the destruction of a rural community in the wake of the militarization of the South.

The promises, opportunities, and problems that accompanied the creation of the Savannah River Plant and other defense-related installations, as well as the impact of the cold war on the South, are part of the larger story of what has come to be known as the South's "second wave" of industrialization. The outlines of the macro view of this "second wave," detailed in many fine studies, reveal an impressive economic and social transformation. Beginning in the New Deal years, but accelerating during World War II, an emerging generation of southern business and political leaders forged a new and lucrative relationship with the federal government. Partly casting aside old antipathies, these neo-Whigs viewed federal aid as indispensable to regional growth and prosperity.[14] Federal dollars became the means by which the South could escape its economic colonialism to the North and acquire the development capital it sorely lacked. The campaign to win federal contracts and installations, as well as to attract industry in general, became a broad-based effort in which local and state political leaders, industrial-development commissions, chambers of commerce, and newspapers joined hands to "sell the South."[15]

As the country moved from depression to war and then from hot war to cold, the nature of southern reliance on federal aid changed. "Increasingly," the historian Bruce Schulman notes, "the representative of the national state in the South was the military."[16] The militarization of southern life accelerated a trend toward urbanization that had been underway since the 1930s.[17] Wartime and especially cold-war urban and suburban growth, however, differed from that which preceded it. For much of the region's history, southern urban growth had been tied to the marketing of staple agriculture, but the economic transformation initiated in the region during the 1930s and expanded during the war and cold-war years greatly attenuated the relationship between city and countryside, affecting the nature and pattern of growth.[18]

Accompanying the creation of the Savannah River Plant was the construction of miles and miles of new suburbs to house the plant's employees. Indeed, Louise Cassels herself ended up a resident of one of these expanding suburbs after she was displaced from her rural community.

Louise Cassels's story—and the history of the forced removal of thousands of South Carolinians—contributes interesting insights to an emerging historiography examining the impact of federal policy and the nature of southern modernization while extending the investigation into the critical cold-war period. George B. Tindall, Pete Daniel, Gavin Wright, and Bruce Schulman, among others, have illustrated the degree to which New Deal policies and wartime imperatives ended the South's colonial economic status and hastened the exodus from the land. Schulman and especially Daniel stress the dark side of this transformation, illustrating how few alternatives were available to modernization's "losers"—unskilled workers and rural inhabitants who were often left behind in progress's wake.[19] A member of a financially secure family, Cassels fared better than most Ellentonians. Still her story of Ellenton hits on the familiar historiographical themes of rapid economic transition and cultural loss that accompanied the arrival of the cold war to the South.

Evacuation Deadline: Midnight, February 29, 1952

Situated approximately two miles from the Savannah River and about twenty-five miles southeast of Augusta, Georgia, Ellenton was the largest community eliminated to make way for the new plant. The small town got its name from James Robert Dunbar Jr. In 1870 Dunbar ceded some property near the Savannah River to the Port Royal–Augusta Railroad, which later became the Charleston and Western Carolina Railroad. The superintendent of railroad construction, who boarded at the Dunbar home, was charmed by Dunbar's nine-year-old daughter, Ellen, and named the depot after her. As a settlement grew up around the junction, Dunbar ceded additional property for streets, and the tiny hamlet became known as "Ellen's Town" or Ellenton.[20]

The small town's subsequent eighty-year history was modest but never static.

This region of the South was no stranger to change. During the nineteenth century, the western counties of South Carolina were in the forefront of technological innovation. The city of Aiken was established in 1835 as a way station along the Charleston to Hamburg railroad, the first railroad in America to provide regular passenger and freight service with steam-powered locomotives.[21] In 1833 the region's first textile mill was constructed in the tiny village of Vaucluse, in Horse Creek Valley in what was then Edgefield District. William Gregg purchased the factory in 1843. Gregg firmly believed that the South's future lay in the development of industry. Two years later, in 1845, Gregg developed, only a few miles from Aiken, the more successful Graniteville Company and village, which stood as the model for the mill-building explosion later in the century.[22]

Despite the relatively poor, sandy soil, the small farming community of Ellenton expanded during the late nineteenth and into the twentieth century. By 1949, 135 families (102 white and 33 black) owned property within the Ellenton town limits.[23] Among them were large landowners, such as the Bush, the Cassels, the Brinkley, and the Dunbar families, who collectively owned thousands of acres. Working many of these acres were the landless—tenants and sharecroppers who, though they might not own land, were nevertheless wedded to it and to the agrarian way of life.

The major cash crop in the region was cotton, but, unlike their Piedmont counterparts, farmers in and around Ellenton were relatively diversified. They grew corn, peanuts, watermelons, cantaloupes, sugarcane, wheat, oats, rye, millet, and rice, either for the market or for their personal consumption.[24] Residents grew or raised much of what they needed. Ellenton resident Annie Polk Linder recalled that the only goods her mother ever bought were sugar, coffee, and rice.[25] Many farmers also kept livestock, to which they fed their wheat, corn, and oats. "My daddy always kept a cow, horses, chickens, hogs, and all those things," Bennie Bowers remembered. "Most everyone had livestock."[26]

Even town folk maintained vegetable gardens and livestock for their family's consumption.[27]

As was typical in agrarian communities, services in Ellenton were sometimes worked out through barter. "You see," resident Carl Brinkley pointed out, "You didn't pay to have [your corn] ground. You'd carry so much corn, say a bushel of corn. Well [the miller] took out his toll at the end. When he ground it out, he kept so much and gave you back yours. . . . You didn't pay. Nobody paid for anything. We just interchanged among ourselves."[28] Although Brinkley's recollection about the absence of cash payment was exaggerated, rural ways of exchange were deeply woven throughout the community. Stephen Harley recalled that Dr. Paul Culbreath, one of the town's two doctors, charged "fifteen dollars and a country ham" to remove his adenoids.[29] The town's other doctor, Dr. Fred C. Brinkley, also owned one of the town's gristmills.[30]

Most of the region's farms had yet to modernize by 1950. Although pesticides had begun to be used in farming with greater frequency, farmers along the Savannah still used traditional labor-intensive methods to combat pests. By 1952 scientists at the Savannah River Plant would be creating plutonium as the nation became locked in a deadly battle for nuclear supremacy with the Soviets. In 1950, however, farmers still waged an exhausting struggle against the boll weevil with nothing more than molasses, poison, and a mop. Nixon Tutt recalled, "We had a poison we would put in molasses, and you would take your mop, go along and hit each piece of cotton on the top, and that boll weevil would get in that and he'd just be dragging on the top up there and just the least bit get on him and it would kill him."[31]

Farming was not the region's sole occupation. Many Ellenton residents who did not farm exclusively worked at the Leigh Banana Crate Company (LBC), the town's only industry.[32] Located on the edge of Barnwell County, LBC crafted containers for transporting fruits and vegetables.[33] It was an enormous enterprise, with its own logging crew and train system. In the 1940s the plant employed around three hundred fifty people during the spring peak season.[34] Those residents not employed by LBC found work in the area's many grist- and sawmills.

As the twentieth century dawned, town life in Ellenton was on the rise. As one historian has noted, although "the farmers established a solid economic foundation for Ellenton to develop upon, . . . it was the local merchants who stimulated and maintained a steady growth in the financial and social status of Ellenton."[35] Ellenton eventually became a trading and commercial district for the surrounding agricultural region, linking the rural hinterland to the outside world.[36] By 1950 Ellenton boasted fifty-six merchants, including several barbershops, a few auto-repair shops, a movie theater, a drugstore, a dry cleaner, a Chevrolet dealership, a post office, several restaurants, and a hotel. On the eve of its destruction the town had completed a new $30,000 school.[37]

Sitting atop Ellenton's merchant class was the Cassels family. Family lore maintains that patriarch Horace Michael Cassels arrived in Ellenton in 1881 at the age of seventeen with only a dollar in his pocket and a puppy in his arms. Cassels found work in one of the local sawmills; within a few years he had saved enough of his wages to buy a farm and build a home. He married Ellen Gazelle Bailey in 1888, and together they had seven children, six of whom survived childhood: Wallace Bailey, William Porter, Horace Michael Jr., Mamie, Augusta Louise, and Sumpter Marion.[38] Cassels expanded his landholdings and developed many commercial enterprises in and around Ellenton. Among these were the Western Carolina Oil and Power Company, which furnished electricity to the town and the surrounding area. When he died in 1931, Cassels's commercial assets included a wholesale grocery business, a seed and feed business, a bank, a funeral parlor, a dairy, and a canning factory. He also owned plantations totaling more than twelve thousand acres.[39]

After his death many of his business operations were taken over by his sons Horace Michael "Mike" Cassels Jr. and Wallace Cassels and son-in-law Arthur Foreman, husband of Mamie Cassels. Rather than split their holdings among the siblings, the family incorporated into the Cassels Co., Inc.[40] Mike Cassels was the public face of the Cassels family and one of Ellenton's leading citizens. He oversaw the family's wholesale and retail businesses and also served as mayor of Ellenton for twenty years.[41] Mike Cassels was best known in town as the owner and operator of the Long Store, a general store so named because it was 210 feet long. Nephew Fielding Foreman remarked that you could buy anything there—"from silk dresses to horse collars." Like other general stores in other small towns, the Long Store became a community gathering place where locals could share information, seek assistance or advice from "Mr. Mike," or just shoot the breeze.[42]

Augusta Louise Cassels, sister to Wallace and Mike, was born in Ellenton in 1899. She attended Shorter College in Rome, Georgia, where she received a degree in music. An accomplished musician, Louise (as she was known) returned to Ellenton, where she lived in the family home with her sister and brother-in-law, Mamie and Arthur Foreman. She taught music and art at Ellenton Grammar School and played the piano and organ in the Ellenton Baptist Church.[43] Friends and relatives remember "Aunt Ease" as "very proper"—the epitome of a schoolteacher. She was tall and slender, always well dressed, and her hair was always fixed.[44] Fielding Foreman, Mamie and Arthur's son, remembered how Louise liked to play classical music in the family's parlor. "That was how I came to learn something about 'The Nutcracker Suite,'" he joked. A much beloved teacher, Miss Louise strove to instruct her students in the finer points of culture. Sid O'Berry recalled fondly how Cassels "introduced [to the class] the works of all the Great Masters—Peter Paul Rubens, Pieter Brueghel, Leonardo da Vinci, Titian, Tintoretto, Renoir, and many others—and explained the mysteries of composition, light, and style, the various periods of art, the architectural designs of Corinthian, Doric, and Ionic—an entire new world in our education."[45] The instruction O'Berry received in Miss Louise's class formed the basis of the knowledge he built upon in his career as a filmmaker. Although Louise Cassels was very proper, no one made the mistake of regarding her as a prim schoolmarm. One close friend recalled that Miss Louise possessed a fiery spirit and did not suffer fools.[46]

At the moment of the arrival of the AEC and Du Pont, then, Ellenton was a small town on the rise. Site planners for the AEC as well as journalists writing about the destruction of Ellenton and the other small communities, however, commented that the residents lived in "rural isolation." They were, in fact, rather well connected to larger urban areas. Although most residents shopped for food and sundries in Ellenton, they traveled to Augusta, Georgia, for their clothing and shoes. The region was well served by the railroad. Both the Charleston and Western Carolina and the Atlantic Coastline trains came through Ellenton twice during the day and once in the evening. Those who preferred the bus could catch the Greyhound at the Blue Goose restaurant.[47] The AEC's use of the term "sufficiently isolated" to describe the proposed area of the Savannah River Plant points to a stark contrast in the understanding of rural space. To the residents the land was alive and productive. Land that was not cultivated could be used for recreation. They hunted in the woods, fished in the rivers and streams, swam in the many lakes, ponds, and creeks, or simply enjoyed the beauty of the landscape. The AEC and Du Pont, on the other hand, regarded this space as "empty," easily cleared and perfect to be used as a buffer—a controllable landscape.[48]

The cold war descended on the small but expanding community of Ellenton in 1950. For days in late summer of that year, residents were aware of strangers in their midst. Men had been spotted surveying the land, boring into the earth, and taking soil samples. What was their business, locals asked themselves? Louise Cassels later recalled that "speculations flew over the community like migrant birds." Some heard reports that they were going to build a glue factory; others claimed it would be an aluminum plant; still others speculated that the engineers were prospecting for oil or kaolin.[49] Jack Harden, son of the town depot agent, told a friend, "My daddy is getting some strange type of telegrams he doesn't understand. . . . They are gonna make tanks or some kind of bullets or some kind of ammunition, he thinks from what these telegrams say." Young Harden did not know where this new plant was going to be located, perhaps "in the Pineywoods, back behind the Blue Goose [restaurant] somewhere."[50] The November 28, 1950, announcement about the creation of the plant answered some questions but posed a new one. How would this new plant affect the residents?

Eight days later, on December 6, 1950, some five hundred individuals and families whose homes fell inside the boundaries of the country's latest cold-war project crowded into the Ellenton school auditorium—whites seated in the middle, blacks lining the room's periphery—to learn their fate. The auditorium could not hold them all, and the crowd spilled outside, leaving anxious residents straining to hear the news. An inhospitable winter drizzle compounded their discomfort.[51] Men in double-breasted suits, officials from Du Pont and the AEC, told the residents they were going to have to evacuate—not just temporarily, but forever. "We came here," Curtis A. Nelson, manager of the new Savannah River Plant operations office stated, "not just to build a war plant but to make things that can be used for peace. We plan to be with you a long time. And to be good citizens of South Carolina."[52]

Anxious residents greeted the news of their impending removal with grim acceptance, comforted only by the fact that theirs was a sacrifice for the greater good of American postwar security. Still, bad feelings festered. In testimony before the House Banking and Currency Committee in February 1951, just a few short months after the announcement of the plant, Congressman John J. Riley of South Carolina's Second District, which included Aiken County, compared the experiences of the residents within the plant area to "the consternation created when General Sherman made his march to the sea in 1864. 'The people there are casualties of the Defense effort. They must accept what is being done to them as their patriotic contribution to the Defense effort of this country.'"[53] Stanley Eubanks of Ellenton expressed more melancholy resignation: "We're sad. We're heart-broken, I guess you could say. But we're not bitter. Our country has asked us to move, and we are going to move. But sometimes we wonder—why did it have to be *Ellenton?*"[54]

Waitin' on the Government Man

Residents did not have the luxury of time to ponder their next move. With the specter of Soviet nuclear capabilities looming and with no end in sight to the Korean conflict, the government seizure of land proceeded at a rapid pace. The job of assessing and acquiring the property was handled by the Land Acquisition Division of the Army Corps of Engineers (COE). COE personnel arrived in western South Carolina on November 29, the day after the plant announcement. Within two weeks their office was fully operational.[55] The COE divided the massive plant site into six priority areas; evacuation dates ranged from March 1, 1951, to June 1, 1952.[56] Property appraisals for the high-priority areas began in December 1950; the first real-estate purchases were made in January 1951. Real-estate property appraisals in Ellenton were started in mid-August 1951.[57]

To answer questions and squelch rumors regarding the land-acquisition and relocation process, the COE distributed regular information bulletins addressed to "Mr. Landowner." Two weeks after the announcement of the plant, affected residents received a bulletin explaining the process. First the government would appraise the property; if the homeowner agreed that the price was fair, he or she would be asked to sign an option contract—"an agreement between you and the Government that you will sell your property to the Government for the price set out in the option." If the government and owner failed to reach an agreement, the matter was turned over to the federal court in a condemnation proceeding.[58] Residents would not be paid for the cost of moving off their property.[59]

Within a very short time residents of the condemned regions had to decide whether to accept the government's offer; they also had to locate new housing in a very tight market. Almost immediately, conflict arose between displaced residents and the federal government. The increasingly defensive nature of the information bulletins indicates the residents' displeasure and suspicion regarding the appraisals. The COE took pains to explain that the land-acquisition policy had withstood legal challenges and "the test of time." It explained what was meant by "fair market value," stating, "the Constitution of the United States provides that just compensation shall be paid for private property taken for public use." Aware that displaced residents viewed it as a federal interloper, the COE pointed out, "most of the men handling this appraisal work are long time residents of this part of South Carolina.

Most of them have many years of experience in this work, are familiar with local conditions, and invariably are inclined to bend over backward to be fair with all the landowners."[60] In fact, of the nineteen local men hired, the majority were from Aiken County, and five were from Ellenton.[61]

Still landowners questioned the process. An aide to U.S. senator Burnet Maybank of South Carolina reported that residents complained of "a difference of fifty percent in [the appraisal of] adjacent farms." He noted that many residents "are not going to accept the offers." Such discrepancies, he surmised, were not the result of "an effort to defraud but incapability [incompetence]."[62] But some citizens suspected a very definite effort to defraud them of the rightful value of their property.[63]

In total the COE acquired more than seventeen hundred separate tracts, nearly half as a result of condemnation.[64] Most small farmers did not have the resources to await the outcome of court proceedings, so they took the settlement and tried to begin life anew. Those with resources hoped for a favorable settlement or jury verdict. Sometimes it took years to settle a dispute. Once a settlement or a judgment was reached, a sizeable percentage went to attorneys' fees. Strom Thurmond—former South Carolina governor and at that time a partner in the Aiken firm Thurmond, Lybrand, and Simons—represented many of the homeowners, as did Aiken attorney Henry Busbee.

The land-condemnation disputes mark an interesting time in Thurmond's already high-profile career. Elected governor in 1946, he entered the office with a reputation as a modernizer, hoping to lure industry and government contracts to the state. By early 1948 he had developed a positive reputation nationwide as a new breed of southern governor. But while he looked to federal spending as a method by which the South could modernize, he drew the line at federal intervention into race relations. In early 1948 Thurmond took the lead in a revolt among Deep South Democrats furious over President Truman's civil rights proposals. Later that year Thurmond ran as the presidential candidate of the States' Rights Democratic Party, coming in a distant third. Two years later, in 1950, he was defeated by incumbent Olin D. Johnston, a strong New Deal Democrat, in a race for the United States Senate.[65]

After leaving the governor's mansion, Thurmond and his wife, Jean, moved to Aiken, where Thurmond took up the practice of law. Although he had returned to private life, Thurmond remained very much a public figure. His comings and goings made front-page news, and he continued to be active in civic affairs. The coming of the bomb plant provided Thurmond a lucrative opportunity with a large political payoff. By winning large returns for landowners, Thurmond strengthened his image as a defender against federal encroachment.

In a trial in which the jury was asked to weigh the opinions of competing expert appraisers, each side took pains to gain any advantage it could. Sympathy for the landowners was the defendants' ace in the hole. Judges instructed the jury not to consider emotional pleas when making its determination; nevertheless Thurmond always managed to pluck the heartstrings of sympathetic jurors, and government attorneys were loathe to object too strenuously so as not to appear callous. In September 1951 Thurmond represented Dr. A. H. Corley in a condemnation proceeding. Corley had refused the government's offer of $57,500 for an 834-acre tract of land. Thurmond urged the jury to consider not only the value of the property, but to determine what constituted just compensation for the sacrifice Corley was being asked to make for the sake of the nation.

> Thurmond: Dr. Corley, I noticed this morning that you appear somewhat disturbed. I just want to ask this question: Has that condition been brought about since the death of your son in the war [World War II]?
> Dr. Corley: Yes.
> Thurmond: Have you been yourself since your son was killed?
> Dr. Corley: No, I haven't.

By revealing to the jury that Dr. Corley had lost a son, Grady, in World War II (a sad fact unrelated to the monetary value of Corley's property), Thurmond implied that the landowner had already made an enormous sacrifice. Thurmond further established that Dr. Corley's other son, A. H. Corley Jr., was employed by the Veterans Administration in Washington, D.C., and could not attend the trial because "his government duties prohibit it." In addition Thurmond reminded the jury that what they were considering was not simply the value of bricks and mortar and land, but compensation for the loss of a way of life.

> Thurmond: You had the boys working on the farm, I believe?
> Corley: That's right.
> Thurmond: I believe you are a believer in the old school of thought of letting the boys work?
> Corley: That's right.
> Thurmond: And putting them out on the farm is the finest place in the world to raise boys, isn't it?
> Corley: Mine did work. I had to work.

Dr. Corley further testified that he bought one tract of land "for my two boys. . . . I wanted to make farmers out of them. Of course, they both got into the Army and one was killed. . . ."[66] His agrarian dream died on the battlefields of World War II. And now, to meet the needs of the cold war, the government was going to strip him of his land. The jury awarded Dr. Corley $70,000, 22 percent above the government's original offer.[67]

Left out entirely from receiving compensation were sharecroppers and tenants. Occasionally one glimpses the fate of a tenant in the legal documents. In his testimony at a trial in which he contested the government's appraisal and offer, landowner Arthur Weathersbee acknowledged that he received a letter from the COE notifying him that the government needed to acquire his property no later than January 15, 1951. "When that [letter] was received, I showed it to all the tenants and all except one moved away immediately."[68] Fielding Foreman commented that the workers who populated the Cassels and Foreman farms likewise "moved all over" when the government seizure began.[69] Sometimes sharecroppers and tenants received compensation for crops. Earl Roberson, a tenant on land owned by Mrs. Clyburn B. Harley, was paid $87.78 for crops destroyed by construction.[70] Waldo K. Keenan was awarded $316.00 for "destruction of crops and loss of labor" related to a tract of land owned by D. C. Bush.[71] R. L. McLean, Nathaniel Bell, and Willie Stallings, tenants, received $431.00 "as the

estimated compensation for the taking of said crops" they had cultivated on the property of Albert A. Weathersbee and Frank Weathersbee Jr.[72]

Researchers and others at the time indicate that the majority of the
nonlandowners were African Americans. A team of researchers from
the University of North Carolina sent to observe the removal and relocation process noted in late 1951 that only "the families of those Negro
wage-earners who could pay their way were among the few non-white
families who appeared to have worked out moving plans."[73] Contem-
porary observers estimated that nearly three thousand landless blacks
would be affected by the government seizure. One reporter observed
that their plight was worsened by the fact that "their life has been
crimped into a vestigial pattern of paternal discrimination." Negro
County Agent T. A. Hammond worried about the fate of the sharecroppers and tenants. "Since this thing happened, fifteen or twenty different counties around have . . . sent requests in . . . for sharecroppers.
I don't know whether these people will go. They're bewildered, used to
depending entirely on the white landowners. They still don't believe
that they won't be loaded into a truck by somebody and moved on
somewhere else."[74] Many of the displaced farmers hoped to get jobs in
the bomb plant.[75] One tenant farmer hoped that his knowledge of the
land would somehow aid him in pursuing work at the new plant. "I
want to be the chauffeur for a government official. I know a good fishing hole to take him to."[76] But knowledge of the land was not prized
in this new enterprise. One journalist noted, "The man who com-
mands a knowledge of the valley's history and of its terrain and waters
is sure to stand in well with his neighbors. To know indisputably where
Mister Walker lived before he lived where he lives now, to be able to
guide a skiff around a submerged stump in the swamp—these have
been immeasurable assets."[77] But no longer.

Indeed, as the magnitude of the events swirling around them began
to register with the residents, they moved from a concern for receiving
just compensation for their property to a realization that they were
about to lose a way of life that could not be bought, could not be
replaced. Would they be able to replicate the intimate relationship to

the land that they had developed over generations? Could that be replaced? Vester Smith, plant superintendent at LBC, was doubtful. "What am I gonna do with my [hunting] dogs? Why, take the eight of them together and they're worth some real money." He figured that most residents in the plant area likewise possessed valuables suited for a pastoral way of life. "Three hundred and seventy-five thousand dollars," he exclaimed. "That's what I figure it at, if you took all the hunting dogs, all the rifles and shotguns, all those good cypress-bottomed fishing boats that nobody but folks around here know how to make anyway. . . . That's for 1,500 families, figuring every man has a shotgun and a dog and a boat, a reel, and some tackle. Now . . . how is the government gonna pay us back for all that? Where else can we get the use of it that we've been getting around here? . . . Where is the government gonna find us swamps like these to hunt and fish in, another Boggy Gut, another Bailey's Pond?"[78]

In addition to the approximately eight thousand living persons, the COE also had to evacuate nearly six thousand departed souls from the region's many graveyards and cemeteries, some of which dated back to the late eighteenth century.[79] The disinterment of the dearly departed upset the residents greatly.[80] Ellenton resident Marion Brinkley recalled his encounter with Lorena Stark, owner of the Blue Goose restaurant, who took steps to conceal her parents' graves from the COE. Stark asked Brinkley, "Marion, what are you going to do 'bout your folks?" Brinkley replied, "Well, I guess I'm going to move them." Stark retorted, "Well, I'm not moving mine!" According to Brinkley, Lorena Stark "got a colored fella and they went back [to the grave site] and she dug a hole, pulled up the tombstones, and buried them." She later told Brinkley, "I'll guarantee you, they'll never find them." And they never did.[81]

In fewer than two years, the region was entirely transformed. Between January 1951 and June 1952, the more than two hundred thousand acres of land desired by the AEC had been cleared of its permanent inhabitants. As bulldozers moved across the landscape, it was divested of its idiosyncratic architectural heritage. The preplant landscape was home to a great variety of vernacular architecture, some of which dated back to the eighteenth century. Someone cruising along the dusty county roads was certain to spot I-houses, shotgun houses, hall-and-parlor houses, cottages, and bungalows. Photographs reveal scores of outbuildings—sheds, corn cribs, privies—some sturdy and well built, some ramshackle.[82] A few buildings residing within the plant's borders were preserved and used by plant personnel; others were moved by their owners; the rest were razed. Highways were clogged with tractor trailers pulling uprooted houses on their way to Aiken, or Jackson, or Williston. Small towns that had once been full of life became ghost towns, occupied only by hungry cats and dogs that had been left behind.[83]

Relocation

While the procedure for assessing and acquiring the property within the boundaries of the site was judicially defined, no similarly clear and consistent line of federal responsibility existed for the removal and resettlement of the displaced population. Those who wished to move their homes to new locations were responsible for contracting with movers.[84] The Farmers Home Administration of the Department of Agriculture set up a relocation center in Aiken but employed only one relocation agent, who, incidentally, was preoccupied with his own relocation efforts.[85] Ultimately the FHA provided financial assistance for fewer than fifty displaced families. Often the prices dispossessed persons received for their property were insufficient to set them up in new locations, leaving many with few palatable options. One farmer, exasperated by the whole process, complained that "I didn't have enough [money] to buy a new piece of land until after I knew how much I'd get for the appraisal. They appraised the neighbors on my right, and the same day they appraised the folks on my left, but they passed me right by. So here I sit. I can't buy any land and all the good land is being bought up every day." Many residents acknowledged that, while they were willing to give up their homes as their patriotic duty, they expected something in return. One woman told a team of investigators that "I'll move now and I'd move again if our country needs it. But it does seem that they could be helping us out more since we didn't ask for this."[86] Although no one tracked their movements systematically, several sources indicate that most residents stayed within the region, moving to existing towns such as Aiken, Jackson, and Williston. Others created new communities. Many displaced persons from the town of Ellenton—120 black and 30 white families—created the town of New Ellenton just outside the plant's perimeter.

The small towns lying outside the boundaries of the plant were soon overwhelmed, not by Ellenton's refugees, but by the Savannah River Plant's more than forty thousand construction workers and permanent operations personnel and their families. The city of Aiken underwent profound changes. Incorporated in 1835, Aiken boasted a population of only seven thousand on the eve of the plant's construction.[87]

Prior to 1950, Aiken existed peacefully, first as a health resort and later as a wealthy enclave, serving the needs and whims of the nation's upper crust. Mrs. Lulie Hitchcock of Long Island came to Aiken in the 1870s after she discovered that Aiken's temperate climate and sandy soil were ideal for raising and training thoroughbreds. Owners of a stable of race horses, Mrs. Hitchcock and her husband brought their equine passion to Aiken. She soon convinced many of her wealthy friends in the horsey set to make Aiken their winter home. Collectively known as the "Winter Colonists," they typically arrived in January and left in April. They built sprawling mansions they called "cottages" and christened with names—some stately, some whimsical—such as Rosehill, Whitehall, Banksia, and Joye Cottage.[88] The cottages lined the beautifully landscaped 150-foot-wide boulevards. Dividing the boulevards were lovely parks, lush with towering magnolias and filled with the riotous color of that magnificent southern trifecta of dogwoods, camellias, and azaleas. The city proudly adopted the slogan "City of Parkways." Most of these broad avenues were still unpaved in 1950, out of consideration for the sensitivity of horses' hooves.[89] The horses of some of the nation's leading racing stables, the majority of which were owned by northerners, wintered in Aiken. Many Kentucky Derby winners held their debuts at the annual Aiken trials on the beautifully laid out Mile Track. When it wasn't extolling its parkways, the city promoted itself as the "Sports Center of the South." Colorful brochures and promotion pieces heralded the region's luxurious accommodations, cultural attainments, and recreation. Polo players began arriving in Aiken shortly after the first recorded game in 1882. For the next half century, Aiken was known as the "Newport of South Carolina," attracting polo players from throughout the "civilized world." The city's entertainment options reflected the desires of the well-heeled winter residents. By the early 1940s Aiken boasted seventeen polo fields but only one movie theater.[90] Even the town's baseball team (representing Aiken in the Tri-County League) was nicknamed the "Tourists."[91] The town's pre-1950s promotional materials liken Aiken's sporting culture to that of European nobility. Aiken prided itself on its flat racing ("the sport of kings"), drag hunts ("colorful replicas of the old type of fox hunting, accompanied by all the thrills and ceremonies so well known in England and other European countries"), steeplechase, and horse shows. Visitors to the area could go horseback riding along the hundreds of miles of bridle paths in Hitchcock Woods, hunt in the many nearby fields, or fish in one of the nearly one thousand ponds and lakes in Aiken County. The region possessed many fine turn-of-the-century hotels whose guests had included such luminaries as Winston Churchill, John Jacob Astor, the wife of actor John Barrymore, and an assortment of dukes, duchesses, barons, countesses, and ambassadors.[92]

By 1953 the city's permanent population had tripled. The city's square mileage had grown 139 percent as a result of suburban annexation and development. Eventually about twenty-one miles of new streets were added to the city. Private developers created twenty-seven new "modern and convenient" subdivisions within commuting distance to the plant. The town hired eighty additional teachers in 1952 and added forty permanent classrooms and thirty-six temporary classrooms. The Savannah River Plant commenced operations in late 1952, and the first shipment of plutonium left the plant in December 1954.[93] The region, which at the close of World War II was categorized as underdeveloped and primarily rural, now represented an important outpost on the frontier of nuclear science as well as an integral component of the national defense state.

Eventually the displaced Ellentonians—"Displaced Persons of World War III," they called themselves—began life anew and accommodated themselves as best they could to the rapid change that had overtaken the region. They settled into their new communities, found new jobs, joined new churches, attended new schools, and made new friends. But they never forgot Ellenton, and Ellenton never completely disappeared. Although the residents and the buildings are gone and nature has reclaimed much of the space, the town's artesian well remains, and one can still spot street curbs through the thick undergrowth. In 2005 former employees of the Savannah River Site and other interested individuals created the Savannah River Site Heritage Foundation, Inc. Its goal is to create a heritage center at the site to educate the public on the technical, social, and ecological impact of the Savannah River Site and the cold war. The foundation also hopes to create a walking trail of the former town of Ellenton, complete with exhibits recognizing the sacrifices of the residents.[94]

Louise Cassels and her sister and brother-in-law eventually moved into their new home in the city of Aiken, purchasing several lots in a new subdivision at the corner of Whiskey Road and Brandy Road.[95] Miss Louise found a new job teaching school, and on Sunday she played the piano and organ in the First Baptist Church of Aiken. Louise Cassels lived long enough to witness the end of the cold war that had changed her life so dramatically. She died in 1999 at the age of ninety-nine.

Notes

1. "Statement by the President on Announcing the First Atomic Explosion in the U.S.S.R., September 23, 1949," in *Public Papers of the Presidents of the United States: Harry S. Truman; Containing the Public Messages, Speeches, and Statements of the President, January 1 to December 31, 1949* (Washington, D.C.: Federal Register Division, National Archives and Records Service, General Services Administration, 1964), 485. Many of the nation's leading scientists opposed the creation of the super bomb on moral and ethical grounds, equating its destructive power with genocide. In November 1949 the members of the Atomic Energy Commission (AEC) recommended against development of the hydrogen bomb. See Samuel F. Wells Jr., "Sounding the

Tocsin: NSC 68 and the Soviet Threat," *International Security* 4 (August 1979): 118. The Joint Chiefs of Staff urged creation of the bomb, arguing that "military considerations" outweighed any moral objections. See "Memorandum by the Joint Chiefs of Staff to the Secretary of Defense," January 13, 1950, *Foreign Relations of the United States, 1950,* vol. 1, *National Security Affairs; Foreign Economic Policy* (Washington, D.C.: U.S. Government Printing Office, 1977), 503–11; Robert J. Donovan, *Tumultuous Years: The Presidency of Harry S Truman, 1949–1953* (New York: Norton, 1982), 150, 152. McMahon is quoted on page 153. "Report to the President by the Special Committee of the National Security Council to the President," January 31, 1950, *Foreign Relations of the United States, 1950,* 1:513–23. For the definitive work on the scientific and political background on the development of the hydrogen bomb, see Richard Rhodes, *Dark Sun: The Making of the Hydrogen Bomb* (New York: Simon & Schuster, 1995).

2. Melvyn P. Leffler, *A Preponderance of Power: National Security, the Truman Administration, and the Cold War* (Stanford: Stanford University Press, 1992), 326; Donovan, *Tumultuous Years,* 78, 83; Wells, "Sounding the Tocsin," 117; Michael J. Hogan, *A Cross of Iron: Harry S Truman and the Origins of the National Security State, 1945–1954* (Cambridge & New York: Cambridge University Press, 1998), 297. For the full text of NSC-68, see *Foreign Relations of the United States, 1950,* 1:234–92.

3. *The Savannah River Plant of the U.S. Atomic Energy Commission* (Aiken, S.C.: U.S. Atomic Energy Commission, Savannah River Operations Office, Office of Public Information, 1963), 3.

4. Daniel Lang, "Camellias and Bombs," *New Yorker,* July 7, 1951, 42.

5. F. Stuart Chapin Jr. and others, *In the Shadow of a Defense Plant: A Study of Urbanization in Rural South Carolina; A Final Report of the Savannah River Urbanization Study* (Chapel Hill: Institute for Research in Social Science, University of North Carolina, 1954), 1. The head of Du Pont's explosives department, H. L. Brown, wrote a memo on November 6, 1950, detailing comparisons between a Paris, Texas, site and the Savannah River location. Brown noted that the Savannah River location had a lower wage scale. Further, the Texas site was occupied by two large cattle ranches, while the Savannah River site was inhabited by "colored agricultural workers" whose "houses are of low value"; presumably they would be easier to dislocate. See Jobie Turner, "Aiken for Armageddon: The Savannah River Site and Aiken, South Carolina" (master's thesis, University of Georgia, 1998), 20–22.

6. United States Atomic Energy Commission, Press Release, November 28, 1950, in Atomic Plant—Miscellaneous file, Burnet R. Maybank Papers, Special Collections, Marlene and Nathan Addlestone Library, College of Charleston, Charleston, South Carolina; U.S. Department of Energy, *Facts and Data on The U.S. Atomic Energy Commission's Savannah River Plant in South Carolina* (Aiken, S.C.: Savannah River Operations Office, 1970), 3–5; *The Savannah River Plant* (Aiken, S.C.: Savannah River Operations Office, U.S. Department of Energy, 1980), 9. The literature on the Korean War is extensive. Standard works include Bruce Cumings, *The Origins of the Korean War*, 2 vols. (Princeton: Princeton University Press, 1981, 1990); William Stueck, *The Korean War: An International History* (Princeton: Princeton University Press, 1995); and Max Hastings, *The Korean War* (London: Joseph, 1987). For the domestic consequences of the Korean War, see especially Paul G. Pierpaoli Jr., *Truman and Korea: The Political Culture of the Early Cold War* (Columbia: University of Missouri Press, 1999), and Hogan, *A Cross of Iron.*

7. *Aiken Standard and Review,* November 29, 1950.

8. Walter Edgar, *South Carolina: A History* (Columbia: University of South Carolina Press, 1998), 503. Mary Beth Reed and others, *Savannah River Site at Fifty,* edited by Barbara Smith Strack (Washington, D.C.: Department of Energy; Stone Mountain, Ga.: New South Associates, 2002), 100–103.

9. Reed, *Savannah River Site,* 136–37.

10. *The Savannah River Plant of the U.S. Atomic Energy Commission,* 5.

11. "The H-Bomb Hits the South," *New Republic,* June 30, 1952, 9.

12. Jordan A. Schwarz, *The New Dealers: Power Politics in the Age of Roosevelt* (New York: Knopf, 1993), 319–20; Bruce J. Schulman, *From Cotton Belt to Sunbelt: Federal Policy, Economic Development, and the Transformation of the American South, 1938–1980* (Durham: Duke University Press, 1994), 136, 140, 149.

13. Reed, *Savannah River Site,* 142. Note that Reed's count differs from Cassels's estimate of six thousand people who were evacuated.

14. The term *neo-Whigs* was coined by Schulman in *From Cotton Belt to Sunbelt,* 128; see also Tony Badger, "Albert Gore and the Politics of the Modern South," paper presented at the Organization of American Historians annual meeting, April 4, 2003; cited with permission of the author.

15. Dewey W. Grantham, *The South in Modern America: A Region at Odds* (New York: HarperCollins, 1995), 265, 270. The phrase is, of course, James Cobb's. See also David R. Goldfield, *Cotton Fields and Skyscrapers* (Baton

Rouge: Louisiana State University Press, 1982), 190; Goldfield, *Region, Race, and Cities* (Baton Rouge: Louisiana State University Press, 1997), 253.

16. Schulman, *From Cotton Belt to Sunbelt,* 135.

17. By 1960, notes Goldfield, "the South was an urban region: more than one-half of the region's population lived in towns and cities" (*Cotton Fields and Skyscrapers,* 143).

18. Goldfield, *Region, Race, and Cities,* 248. Goldfield notes that during the war years, "The urban South was changing its basic function, from serving as a market for surrounding countryside to serving as a magnet for economic opportunity" (249).

19. George B. Tindall, *The Emergence of the New South, 1913–1945* (Baton Rouge: Louisiana State University Press, 1967); Pete Daniel, *Breaking the Land: The Transformation of Cotton, Rice, and Tobacco Cultures since 1880* (Urbana: University of Illinois Press, 1985); Schulman, *From Cotton Belt to Sunbelt;* Gavin Wright, *Old South, New South: Revolutions in the Southern Economy since the Civil War* (New York: Basic Books, 1986); Nan Woodruff, "Mississippi Delta Planters and Debates over Mechanization, Labor, and Civil Rights in the 1940s," *Journal of Southern History* 60 (May 1994): 263–84; Jack Temple Kirby, *Rural Worlds Lost: The American South, 1920–1960* (Baton Rouge: Louisiana State University Press, 1987); Neil R. McMillen, ed., *Remaking Dixie: The Impact of World War II on the American South* (Jackson: University Press of Mississippi, 1997).

20. Ellenton was officially incorporated on December 24, 1880. See Tonya Algerine Browder and Richard David Brooks, *Memories of Home: Reminiscences of Ellenton,* Savannah River Archaeological Research Heritage Series 2, Occasional Papers of the Savannah River Archaeological Research Program Community History Project (Columbia: Savannah River Archaeological Research Program, South Carolina Institute of Archaeology and Anthropology, University of South Carolina, 1996), vii, 3, 6.

21. *South Carolina: The WPA Guide to the Palmetto State* (1941; reprint, Columbia: University of South Carolina Press, 1988), 160; Louis Cassels, *Coontail Lagoon: A Celebration of Life* (Philadelphia: Westminster Press, 1974), 47.

22. Broadus Mitchell, *William Gregg: Factory Master of the Old South* (1928; reprint, New York: Octagon, 1966), 11–14, 33–75. For a thoughtful examination of the competing economic forces that shaped the Savannah River Valley of western South Carolina, see Tom Downey, *Planting a Capitalist South:*

Masters, Merchants, and Manufacturers in the Southern Interior, 1790–1860 (Baton Rouge: Louisiana State University Press, 2006).

23. Browder and Brooks, *Memories of Home: Reminiscences of Ellenton*, 11.

24. Ibid., 12.

25. Ibid., 14.

26. Ibid., 21.

27. Ibid., 14.

28. Ibid.

29. Ibid., 62.

30. Ibid., 13.

31. Ibid., 12.

32. George McMillan, "The H-Bomb's First Victims," *Reporter*, March 6, 1951, 19.

33. Lucius Sidney O'Berry, *Ellenton, S.C.: My Life, Its Death*, ed. Richard David Brooks and Tonya Algerine Browder, Savannah River Archaeological Research Heritage Series 4, Occasional Papers of the Savannah River Archaeological Research Program Community History Project (Columbia: Savannah River Archaeological Research Program, South Carolina Institute of Archaeology and Anthropology, University of South Carolina, 1999), 134.

34. O'Berry, *Ellenton*, 156n91.

35. Browder and Brooks, *Memories of Home: Reminiscences of Ellenton*, 43.

36. Ibid., 44; Louis and Charlotte Cassels, *An Inquiry into the Origins of the Cassels Family of Ellenton, S.C.* (Bethesda, Md.: privately printed, 1971), 1.

37. Browder and Brooks, *Memories of Home: Reminiscences of Ellenton*, 50, 57; *Aiken Standard and Review*, December 6, 1950, 1.

38. Cassels and Cassels, *Inquiry*, 1–2. According to county deed records, Ellen G. Cassels was the first in the family to purchase property—one-quarter acre in Ellenton for fifty dollars in 1900. See Direct Index to Titles, A–Mc, 1872–1913, and Title Book D1, p. 376, Register of MESNE Conveyances, Aiken County, Aiken County Government Complex, Aiken, South Carolina. H. M. Cassels first appears in the deed books in 1903. See Direct Index to Titles, A–Mc, 1872–1913, and Title Book L1, p. 342.

39. O'Berry, *Ellenton*, 142n57; Cassels and Cassels, *Inquiry*, 1.

40. Cassels and Cassels, *Inquiry*, 1; Fielding Foreman, telephone interview with the author, November 18, 2005.

41. Cassels and Cassels, *Inquiry*, 2.

42. Fielding Foreman, interview. The records of the dissolution of the corporation list thirty-two separate properties and businesses owned in common by the Cassels/Foreman family. See Title Book 127, pp. 292–97.

43. Cassels and Cassels, *Inquiry*, 3; *Shorter College Alumni Directory*, 1999 (White Plains, N.Y.: Bernard C. Harris, 1999), 23; Browder and Brooks, *Memories of Home: Reminiscences of Ellenton*, 93.

44. Arthur Ashley Foreman III, telephone interview with the author, October 24, 2005; Fielding Foreman, interview; Sonya Mazzell, telephone interview with the author, November 15, 2005.

45. O'Berry, *Ellenton*, 70; Fielding Foreman, interview.

46. Mazzell, interview.

47. Browder and Brooks, *Memories of Home: Reminiscences of Ellenton*, 63, 64.

48. Reed, *Savannah River Site*, 133.

49. Lang, "Camellias and Bombs," 47–48; McMillan, "The H-Bomb's First Victims," 18; *Aiken Standard and Review*, December 6, 1950, 1.

50. Browder and Brooks, *Memories of Home: Reminiscences of Ellenton*, 164.

51. McMillan, "The H-Bomb's First Victims," 18; Reed, *Savannah River Site*, 140.

52. McMillan, "The H-Bomb's First Victims," 19. *Aiken Standard and Review*, December 8, 1950, 1.

53. *Aiken Standard and Review*, February 9, 1951.

54. Eubanks quoted in Booton Herndon, "That Others May Live," *Redbook*, March 25, 1951, 80.

55. Reed, *Savannah River Plant*, 147.

56. South Atlantic Division, Corps of Engineers, Information Bulletin No. 5, January 15, 1951, in Atomic Plant—General Information File, Maybank Papers.

57. Chapin, *In the Shadow of a Defense Plant*, 68; *Aiken Standard and Review*, January 31, 1951.

58. South Atlantic Division, Corps of Engineers, Information Bulletin No. 1, Dec. 13, 1950, in Atomic Plant—General Information File, Maybank Papers.

59. Ibid.

60. See South Atlantic Division, Corps of Engineers, Information Bulletin No. 6, January 29, 1951, in Atomic Plant—General Information File, Maybank Papers; and Information Bulletin No. 11, n.d., in Atomic Plant—Land Investigation File, Maybank Papers.

61. Reed, *Savannah River Site,* 147.

62. Dick Richardson to Maybank, March 18, 1951, Atomic Plant—Land Investment File, Maybank Papers.

63. See Cassels, *Coontail Lagoon,* 72–73.

64. Reed, *Savannah River Site,* 155, 154. It should be noted that not all property disputes went to trial. Often, when a clear title could not be readily established, property was included in a "Complaint in Condemnation and Declaration of Taking." Once clear title was established, many of these property owners accepted the government's offers. See, for example, *U.S. v. 5139.5 acres of land, more or less, situate in Aiken and Barnwell Counties, South Carolina, and A. H. Corley et al., and unknown owners,* Civil Action 2758, Tract No. A-52, Order and Judgment, December 23, 1953, box 267, District Court of the United States for the Eastern District of South Carolina, Aiken Division, Record Group 21, National Archives and Records Administration, Southeastern Center, Atlanta, Georgia.

65. For Strom Thurmond's presenatorial career, see Kari Frederickson, *The Dixiecrat Revolt and the End of the Solid South, 1932–1968* (Chapel Hill: University of North Carolina Press, 2001).

66. Civil Action 2758, *United States v. 5139.5 acres of land . . . ,* Tracts No. A-45 and A-63, Dr. A. H. Corley and A. H. Corley Jr., Landowners, Testimony, September 27–28, 1951, pp. 7, 12, 9, 82, box 269, RG 21.

67. Civil Action 2758, *United States v. 5139.5 acres of land . . . ,* Tract No. A-45, Verdict, September 28, 1951, box 269, RG 21.

68. Ibid., Tract No. A-60, Sleepy Hollow Farms, testimony, October 1–3, 1951, p. 19, box 269, RG 21.

69. Fielding Foreman, interview.

70. Civil Action 2834, *United States v. 6945.3 acres of land . . . ,* Tract No. H-748, Order and Judgment, August 16, 1951, box 277, RG 21.

71. Civil Action 3824, *United States v. 6945.3 acres of land . . . ,* Tract No. H-709, Order and Judgment, August 8, 1951, box 277, RG 21. The owner, D. C. Bush, received $21,442 for the 151.5-acre plot; the government's original offer was $17,500. See Final Judgment, October 13, 1952.

72. Civil Action 2758, *United States v. 5139.5 acres of land . . . ,* Tract No. A-60, Order and Judgment, June 21, 1951, box 267, RG 21.

73. Chapin, *In the Shadow of a Defense Plant,* 69.

74. McMillan, "The H-Bomb's First Victims," 20 (both quotations).

75. "The Displaced," *Time,* December 11, 1950, 22.

76. Lang, "Camellias and Bombs," 48.

77. McMillan, "The H-Bomb's First Victims," 17.

78. Ibid., 19.

79. Reed, *Savannah River Site,* 154.

80. Mazzell, interview.

81. Browder and Brooks, *Memories of Home: Reminiscences of Ellenton,* 162.

82. See, for example, Civil Action 2758, *United States v. 5139.5 acres of land . . . ,* Tract No. D-308, Photographic Exhibits, box 269, RG 21. See also Reed, *Savannah River Site,* 155–56; and Melanie A. Cabak and Mary M. Inkrot, *Old Farm, New Farm: An Archaeology of Rural Modernization in the Aiken Plateau, 1875–1950,* Savannah River Archaeological Research Papers 9, Occasional Papers of the Savannah River Archaeological Research Program (Columbia, S.C.: Savannah River Archaeological Research Program, South Carolina Institute of Archaeology and Anthropology, University of South Carolina,1997), 23–25.

83. Louise Cassels, *The Unexpected Exodus* (Columbia: University of South Carolina Press, 2007), 87.

84. Chapin, *In the Shadow of a Defense Plant,* 67.

85. Deborah J. Holland, "Steward of World Peace, Keeper of Fair Play: The American Hydrogen Bomb and Civil Rights, 1945–1954" (Ph.D. diss., Northwestern University, 2002), 51.

86. Chapin, *In the Shadow of a Defense Plant,* 67, 75–76.

87. "The Atom," *Time,* December 11, 1950, 22.

88. Dorothy Kelly MacDowell, *An Aiken Scrapbook: A Picture Narrative of Aiken and Aiken County, South Carolina* (Aiken, S.C.: privately printed, 1982).

89. Lang, "Camellias and Bombs," 40.

90. *South Carolina: The WPA Guide,* 159.

91. See, for example, *Aiken Standard and Review,* June 16, 1952, 5.

92. Register, Willcox Hotel, Aiken County Historical Museum, Aiken, South Carolina.

93. Reed, *Savannah River Site,* 131, 236–40; Curtis A. Nelson to John A. May, March 25, 1953, box 9, Savannah River Project file, General Subject file, James F. Byrnes Papers, South Carolina Department of Archives and History, Columbia.

94. J. Walter Joseph, "SRS Heritage Foundation," July 31, 2005, in the author's possession.

95. Title Book 124, p. 298; "Subdivision Surveyed for W. H. Cato and Mrs. J. W. Houth," 1946, Miscellaneous Deed Book 26, p. 139, RMC, ACGC. Ironically, one block away from Cassels's Aiken home is the office of the Citizens for Nuclear Technology Awareness.

Ellenton School. Courtesy of the Savannah River Archaeological Research Program, South Carolina Institute of Archaeology and Anthropology, University of South Carolina

Ellenton. Courtesy of the Savannah River Site, U.S. Department of Energy

Leigh Banana Crate Company. Courtesy of the Savannah River Archaeological
Research Program, South Carolina Institute of Archaeology and Anthropology,
University of South Carolina

Jean's Place café, the theater, and a store. Courtesy of the Savannah River Archaeological Research Program, South Carolina Institute of Archaeology and Anthropology, University of South Carolina

The Blue Goose restaurant. Courtesy of the Savannah River Archaeological Research Program, South Carolina Institute of Archaeology and Anthropology, University of South Carolina

INTRODUCTION TO
THE FIRST EDITION

My Aunt Louise and I have a special bond which was wrought for us by the United States Post Office Department. For half a century, we have been getting each other's mail. Since only the letter "e" distinguishes "Louis Cassels" from "Louise Cassels," you can see how easily the two names may be confused. It didn't matter terribly when I was a small boy growing up in our home town of Ellenton, South Carolina, and my Aunt Louise was a young teacher in the public school there. If the magazine was *Boy's Life,* we knew it belonged to me, and if it was *The NEA Journal,* it was meant for her.

As we grew older, things got a bit more complicated. My aunt became more prominent in her profession, and I got to be mildly notorious in mine. She definitely got the worst of it in the continuing confusion of our identities because whereas I might receive a warm letter praising me for some achievement in education, she would get crank letters from my severest critics because of some story I had written for the newspapers.

I mention all this to explain why the event is of particular significance to us to have *both* of our names appear together on the jacket of this book. For once, nobody can attribute the project to the wrong Cassels; we are jointly involved:

My involvement, of course, is minuscule compared to that of my aunt. She lived through the traumatic days described so vividly in this book, while I was far away in Washington, D.C., coming back only for an occasional visit to the little town of Ellenton as it underwent its death throes. When the ordeal was over, I, along with other members of the family, urged Aunt Louise to write down her memories of it while they were fresh. This book is the result of our persuasion.

You'll find it a warm, anecdotal, engrossing story of what happened to a quiet little town and its people when they suddenly found themselves in the way of a $1,300,000,000 atomic plant. All of the stories are true, and all of the people are real, although my aunt, out of sensitivity for other people's feelings, has used fictitious names for a few minor characters who play less than heroic parts in the story. My father was the Mike Cassels who is mentioned several times in the text. He died within five years of his transplantation from Old Ellenton, and it is a poignant regret to me that he could not have read this account by the kid sister whom he greatly loved.

Louis Cassels
Senior Editor,
United Press International

THE UNEXPECTED EXODUS

Dedicated to the memory of Ellenton
and to the courageous people who sacrificed their town
in the spirit of patriotism

Chapter I

ELLENTON

In the fall of 1950, an air of excitement pervaded the sleepy little town of Ellenton nestling contentedly in South Carolina's historical lowlands near the Savannah River. For several months its easygoing folk had noticed unusual events happening in and around their community; and they knew they were significant: Why were boring crews circulating the town? Why were soil samples needed? Why were strangers continually coming and going? Since no one seemed to understand these mysterious missions, speculations flew over the community like migrant birds. The most likely conclusions were: either oil had been discovered or useful minerals found in the soil.

But regardless of what might come, the people would welcome it to spur their lagging economy and increase the population. Since this agricultural community had few natural resources to attract newcomers, it suffered from a stunted growth. And even though industry was slowly moving in, it wasn't sufficient to give the impetus needed for the progress the people longed for. Now after all these years Ellenton was fast becoming a nonagenarian; [person aged 90-99.] the population had barely reached a thousand. So, like excited and impatient children waiting for Santa on Christmas Eve, the people waited for developments.

Ellenton was born when the Charleston & Western Carolina Railroad was built in the 1870's. The section that ran from Charleston, South Carolina, to Augusta, Georgia, cut through Robert Jefferson Dunbar's plantation near his big three-storied home where the superintendent of construction, Mr. Millett, boarded. He became so charmed with Mr. Dunbar's attractive nine-year-old daughter, Ellen, that he requested the company to name the station near the Upper Three Runs neighborhood for her.

Soon people from several other adjoining vicinities, Four Mile and Steel Creek among them, came to live by the railroad to enjoy its conveniences. These were the aborigines: A religious, cultured, and educated group.

No wonder the descendants were proud of their heritage. They loved their home town, too; for even though it was small it wasn't obscure, but well-known for the most outstanding asset any place could possess—its people. Their friendly, hospitable way of life stamped itself forcefully upon outsiders; they, too, enjoyed the community.

It was also outstanding as a pleasure-loving town: Many social affairs stemmed through the women's and men's clubs. Creeks, lakes, and ponds dotted the countryside, furnishing pleasure for fishing, swimming, boating, and picnics. And the muddy Savannah River was an old, trusted friend giving happiness to young and old. Perhaps the generation that enjoyed an annual boat trip on *Katy*, running from Augusta to Savannah, Georgia, taking almost a week for the round trip, felt closest to her. When a loud whistle blew on a summer morning, everyone knew it was *Katy* nearing Point Comfort, the port of departure for this well-chaperoned group.

Ellenton's setting was picturesque. Nature had beautified it with many stately trees: Different varieties of oaks, magnolias, pines, Carolina cherries, and hollies towered over the town. Flowers grew abundantly. But the residential and business sections weren't segregated and that marred its overall beauty. It reminded one of a ragged person with well-formed features and a fine physique. Naturally visitors and newcomers quickly noticed this hodge-podge plan; but soon, like all old-timers, their eyes adjusted to the sight, and they failed to see its ugliness.

This was my home town. I'd lived here most of my life in the ancestral home and loved every inch of it. Even though the lot was large—several acres in all—the two-storied frame house, filled by six children, sat close to the street and near the right boundary, leaving enough space on the left to build another house. I suppose my father had good reasons for placing it there since he was a very practical person; anyhow, he used every foot of land to provide health and happiness for the family.

Our back yard was an arena of action where the older and younger children frequently waged battles. Generally, the older ones initiated them by teasing or domineering the younger. A playhouse, built for my older sister, Mamie, and me, often served as a bulwark. And a chinaberry tree growing in front of it provided berries for ammunition, and a means of climbing to the roof. When battles got too hot, the younger children would lock themselves in the playhouse. Then when everything was quiet and we thought the older ones had gone, we'd peep out only to have a volley of chinaberries pelt us from the roof. The fighting would last until my mother would step to the back porch and, like a general, order peace.

Directly behind the playground were the stables. Our pony, Julius Caesar, was as stubborn a creature as anyone ever dealt with. Even though he was gentle, he ruled—I suppose that's why his name was Julius Caesar. We'd have to coax him from the stables and the yard; even after getting him to the road, he'd poke along. Then suddenly, with no warning whatsoever, he'd turn around and give us a fast trot home.

On the left of our house was a large vegetable garden—not a foot too much for our big family though. Just the narrow front yard had any flowers; but it was chock-full.

As the years passed the older children married, and the younger ones went to college. Then my mother, who had always had a passion for flowers and now had more leisure time, happily turned her attention to gardening. My father delighted in carrying out her dreams and since she became an expert at landscaping, her plans called for many changes:

The vegetable garden replaced the stables—no longer needed. And tall shrubbery hid it from sight. Instead of the wooden fence, an evergreen wall surrounded the lot. Then Father bought property adjoining the boundary line on the right to give the house better symmetry. And the narrow front yard planted in cut flowers became a lawn with stepping stones to point the way to either side of the garden. With these changes, the natural result was a U-shaped garden.

As if overnight, Mother changed the new, weedy lot into a formal English garden. A brick walk extending up the middle and one across its width intersected at the center where a birdbath stood. This divided the lawn into four rectangular beds, edged with dwarf boxwood and filled with low-growing perennials. The corners near the birdbath curved in to form a circular pathway around it. At the head of the middle path was a curved brick-cement bench where one could sit and enjoy the vista.

At the end of this garden a pergola, heavy with a purple wisteria vine, stretched across the plot where the U began to curve. It connected the English garden with our once-upon-a-time active playground that now was a tranquil lawn looking like a green, placid sea. Deodara cedars resembling giant Christmas trees, Burfordii hollies, tea olives, and many varieties of camellias flanked the lawn and guarded it like sentinels. And tucked happily in the middle of this stately setting sat the playhouse, looking like a miniature home. Mother refused to part with it for it symbolized the happiness of our youth.

But Mother's greatest achievements in loveliness were in the gardens on the left: Behind a variety of tall shrubs and flowering bushes that extended across the lawn was a secluded rectangular enclosure walled in by similar shrubs. A pathway, through a natural opening on the inner side of the garden, led under an arc-shaped cedar arbor with a profusion of yellow Lady Banksia roses.

Opposite the arbor stood a slightly curved rockery about twenty feet long and five feet high. Hardy perennials and branches of creeping junipers fell gracefully from the top, which was constructed for plantings. Water rippled over the rockery and made its way into a heart-shaped lily pool bordered with dwarf evergreens and a sprinkling of blooming annuals. On either side of the pool and arbor were beds filled with roses of charming fragrance and fascinating colors. Beyond the pool on the outward side was another natural opening that led into the most extensive part of the entire garden. Here was one of the ideal sites for a panoramic view.

Two entrances from the front yard gave the appearance of two gardens in one. From the corner of the house, a four-foot brick walk paralleled the side-screened porch and adjoining solarium. Bordering either side were white candytuft and pink dwarf azaleas. In front of each brick pilaster grew stately camellia bushes. The walk then became the outer part of a brick patio used as a side entrance into the solarium. Beyond this outdoor living room with its white wrought-iron benches were masses of tall azalea bushes with red and white blooms in season. With a graceful white dogwood serving as a background, a gazing globe mounted on an old millstone reflected the colorful scene.

The other entrance was a large rustic arbor covered with a massive yellow jessamine vine. Double gates built within opened into the main entrance of this spacious lawn. In the middle was a little wrought-iron boy standing on a tall cement base. He sprayed water high into the air which formed oval shapes before falling into the large round pool, circled with spreading junipers and other colorful drawf bushes.

[7]

Situated at the far end of the garden and in direct line with the pool, a small cedar arbor, veiled in yellow jessamine was snuggled among graduating shrubs and flowering bushes. Since this particular spot had served as an altar, it held a great deal of family sentiment: It was here that Mamie's daughter, Ellen, was married.

Even before my mother passed away, she'd given the ancestral home to Mamie and me and had the property entailed during our lifetime. She had said, "I've had so much happiness with your father in making this garden and comfort in it, too, after he died. Now I've had joy in perfecting it for Ellen's wedding and in the thoughts of leaving it for your future enjoyment. And *no one* can take it from you."

Five years later this thirty-year-old garden had become our inheritance to keep and enjoy. Love for God's nature had inspired the making, and every flower, bush, and tree represented part of that love in fulfilling the plans as a whole.

Thanksgiving holidays had come. The college crowd and out-of-town relatives had arrived. Many friends had also come to hunt, for Ellenton was a hunter's town. In season there were birds, deer, 'possums, 'coons, rabbits, squirrels, and foxes. The weather was fair, but unseasonably cold—nine above zero the day after Thanksgiving. However, excitement was at such a high pitch over "what's coming?" that the popular subjects of hunting and weather slid into secondary topics. The visitors shared our excitement; for they loved this typical low-country southern town with its hospitality. "Promise us," they begged, "the minute you find out what it is, you'll let us know." We solemnly promised.

On the night of November 27, Mamie, Arthur, her husband, and I dropped in to see Mike, our brother, to talk about unsubstantiated reports circulating the town.

With his hands in his pockets, Mike was pacing back and forth in front of us. "Strangers galore were in town today, but I couldn't get a *word* out of 'em," he said. Then, he stopped and looked at us with his forehead puckered in deep thought. "How much longer, do you suppose, we'll have to wait before we'll hear something definite?"

"I hope tomorrow, for I can't wait another day to know what it's all about," Arthur replied, gripping the arms of his chair in a nervous manner.

Suddenly, I blurted out, "I've an uncanny feeling it's something that'll change our entire way of life!"

"There you go with that intuitive mind of yours," Mamie said, amused at my purported "sixth sense."

I looked at Mamie, shaking my head, "Everything is too secretive to suit me."

We didn't have to wait long. At that very hour a number of officials from the Atomic Energy Commission and E. I. du Pont de Nemours Company were in Augusta, Georgia, just across the Savannah River from South Carolina, making plans for the announcement the next day.

At the ten o'clock recess in the centralized elementary school where I taught, all the teachers, except those on duty, had gathered in the teachers' lounge. "I heard last night an aluminum plant . . ." A knock on the door interrupted Mary, the first grade teacher. "I'll get it," she said, jumping up and opening it. Then she turned and looked at me. "It's for you, Weezer, you're wanted on the phone."

I almost ran to the office, for Mamie had promised to call if she heard anything. My hands trembled as I picked up the receiver. "We hear an H-Bomb plant is coming," she said, in a highly excited voice.

"An H-Bomb plant? We don't want *that*. It's dangerous!" I replied, as though she could change the situation.

"Well, that's the report anyway. I'll let you know if I hear anything more."

Disappointed, I returned to the lounge. "Mamie says it's rumored an H-Bomb plant is coming."

"Oh, no!" Lib said, horrified.

I raved on as though I was speaking for them—and I was. "We don't want Ellenton to have a part in destroying people and places. Our town is peace-loving. We'd rather stay small than have an H-Bomb plant here."

"Who's responsible for this?" Betty asked, looking at each of us as if she were trying to find the culprit. No one could answer that question. The bell rang; recess was over. We returned to our schoolrooms a displeased, disappointed group.

Two hours later a little after twelve o'clock, Tuesday, November 28, 1950, Ellenton's doom was sealed. The radio sent out a blaze of words so unbelievable that people couldn't comprehend the meaning at the time:

"The United States Atomic Energy Commission today announced that its new production plants to be designed, built, and operated by the E. I. du Pont de Nemours Company of Wilmington, Delaware, will be located in Aiken and Barnwell counties, South Carolina, near the Savannah River. About 250,000 acres will be acquired for the site. Exact boundaries remain to be determined. The new site will be known as the Savannah River Plant.

"As was noted by the President last July in asking Congress to appropriate $260,000,000 to start construction, these additional plants, like the existing facilities, will provide materials which can be used either for weapons or for fuels potentially useful for power purposes.

"The site was chosen by the Commission after a four-month study of more than 100 sites by the du Pont Company and AEC engineers with the assistance of other federal agencies . . .

"To make way for the plants and the surrounding security and safety zone, it will be necessary for about 1,500 families to relocate in the next 18 months. The Federal-State Agricultural Agencies are organizing to give help to the families who must relocate. The first families affected will be those in areas 1 and 2 on the map. These general areas will be vacated at an early date to make way for construction. . . ."

Ellenton and Dunbarton, only half as large as Ellenton, had become the first incorporated communities ever taken over by the U. S. Government for an atomic facility. Also included were other small communities: Hawthorne, Meyers Mill, Robbins and Leigh.

The school didn't hear the death sentence nor was it announced to the teachers, but a few heard it soon after in different ways. I'd just returned from lunch and seated my sixth-grade children, that is, all but one, who had special permission to have his lunch at his pretty, new-brick home facing the school across the street. "You're late, Robert," I said, as he entered the room.

Robert disregarded my remark and stood still. His big blue eyes, opened wider than usual, had a horrified stare. "Didya know," he said, as though he were a robot, "everybody's gotta move out of Ellenton?" He hesitated then continued, "Even the dead—a bomb plant is coming."

Not a child spoke. Neither did I—I couldn't. I froze. How long the tableau lasted I've no knowledge. But Robert's next remark helped me back to reality. "Mom said the announcement came over the radio after twelve."

"Who made it?" I managed to ask, and backed a step to lean against the front of my desk.

"The Government—and Mr. Mike, too. He said we hated to give up our town, but we would, if it's necessary to save our country."

The mention of my brother's name sent blood surging to my head. "Where was he when he said that?"

"In Augusta, over the radio."

I couldn't understand why Mike was speaking over the radio. Later I found out the AEC officially informed him and other town officials of the Government's intentions an hour before the public or press knew it. They also asked him to express his feelings about sacrificing his home town for our country.

Robert walked mechanically to his desk and sat down. His announcement whirled around and around in my mind. Everyone had to move—even the dead would need new resting places. Suddenly, a thought jumped at me: Mother's garden! And she had said, "*No one* can take it from you."

But I didn't have time to linger with my thoughts; my stunned children began coming to life. They bombarded me with questions I couldn't answer: Why was an H-Bomb plant coming to Ellenton? When would they have to move? Where would they go?

I finally dragged my leaden feet around the desk and sat down, allowing the children to question Robert while I resumed my thinking. Mamie had said she'd let me know if she heard anything more. Why hadn't she called? And where was she and how had she taken the news? Where was the principal? Why hadn't he come to tell us? The children were upset and I was in despair. I looked at my watch. It was over an hour before time to dismiss. In desperation I said, "Let's go on with our work. When we get home we'll learn all about it."

Naturally their interest in school work was at a low ebb; time seemed to stand still. But in some sort of fashion, I tried to work as though nothing had happened. At least it was the best steadying force I could find for the present. I wonder now how I ever did it.

After school, I stopped long enough to see if Mary had heard. We'd taught together all our teaching lives, and a close bond of friendship existed between us. I didn't have to ask. "Weezer," she sobbed, hugging me, "it's made me sick." Her emotions reached such a high tension that afternoon, she became physically ill.

When I got home I found Mamie sitting alone in the living room. "You've heard?" she said, looking at me.

"Yes, I'm still numb," I said, dropping into my favorite rocking chair.

"I'm stunned, too. The very foundations I'd thought permanent were swept away in a minute's time. When I heard the announcement, everything material seemed to mock me—even the draperies as they receded with the wall. The floor sank beneath me and my good old sofa sank along with it." Mamie gently patted her favorite napping place.

"I told you last night I had a feeling our way of life was about to change. This is *one* time my analytical mind proved to be right." Momentarily I became frightened over my own premonition.

"Yes, you were right this time." Suddenly, Mamie pushed herself to the edge of the sofa and started speaking like a preacher, "You know this experience is shocking, but one I'll always treasure. No man, no plans of the Government, no material things can take God from a person who trusts Him." My sister meant that; in spite of the many hardships we had to endure, she marched onward like a Christian soldier.

"If ever an experience has taught that lesson, I'm sure it's this one. But what a hard way to learn it," I said, shaking my head.

Mamie looked out the window and her eyes became thoughtful. She spoke quietly now. "We'll miss our beautiful garden more than anything."

A lump rose in my throat. I just nodded as I looked at the camellia bushes loaded with flowers hurt by the recent cold weather.

"And we thought *no one* could take it! I'm glad Mother doesn't have to experience this," Mamie said.

"That's something for which we ought to be thankful. Do you feel like someone in the family has just died?" I asked, rubbing my hand over my aching forehead.

"Yes, I do; and doom is certainly upon every home in Ellenton." Mamie turned to look at Arthur coming in the door.

"Well, we're certainly in a mess," he said, as he sat down looking tired from the emotional strain of the day. "Everyone is upset. Just how the people are coming out financially is something no one knows yet."

"What's the first move?" Mamie asked.

"Tomorrow night the Government's representatives will talk to the people, that is, to a representative from each family, at the school auditorium to explain the procedures of acquiring the homes and land."

Shivers ran through my body when I heard the words, "acquiring the homes." "How long before we'll have to leave?" My voice sounded like one asking the doctor how much longer can a loved one live.

"We're not in the areas that will have to move in the next six weeks I'm glad to say. We may . . ."

The phone ringing interrupted our first brief family discussion since the night before. Not until midnight were we free from answering local and out-of-town calls that came from as far west as Chicago. Ellenton's plight grieved them. They hadn't thought of it as just another small town—true it was—but one that had charm and personality. Its individuality had won the hearts of surprisingly many people who had experienced living or visiting there. Miss Josephine Erwin—"Miss Jo" to her friends—a lifetime friend and visitor from Hartsville, South

Carolina, had just returned from spending Thanksgiving holidays in Ellenton. The shocking news made her ill for several weeks.

Next morning the alarm woke me at seven. For a moment I couldn't get my bearings; then reality overwhelmed me like a wave rolling over a beach. Ellenton was doomed. I shuddered at the thought. How I wished I could sleep through this terrible experience ahead of everyone. Slowly, I got out of bed and mechanically began to dress. School teaching, like show business, must go on.

Although past excitement and the strain of yesterday had drained me physically, my overactive mind wouldn't slow down. All day long I kept contrasting the weather and the happenings of last Wednesday with that of today, making my feelings even more poignant.

A week ago the weather was extremely cold for South Carolina, but it hadn't affected anyone's plans for the Thanksgiving holidays. It seemed preparations went on with more zest than usual. No doubt, though, the people's exhilaration over the expected industry was closely linked with their high spirits. Now today, the weather was normal—just a little on the warm side. But the people, broken in spirit, were in despair; they felt trapped. Overnight the Government had thrown them into a new era—the era of a slow, painful exodus, one they hadn't anticipated.

Then tonight, so different from last Wednesday night when guests and relatives were arriving, the Government would meet the people for a question and answer session. Their anxiety over not receiving just compensation for their property had reached a high pitch. This meeting was mandatory to allay fears—at least I hoped it would. Or was it just another way for the Government to tell the people how and when they'd have to pull up their grassroots to move into someone else's world, and let them have the beloved place to manufacture materials for atomic weapons.

When eight o'clock finally crept in, people crowded the school auditorium, even standing against the walls, in the aisles, and barely within the doors. Naturally the first question asked was what concerned everyone most: What was the Government's acquisition policy for land and property?

The Government stated it was the same as that followed for any other Government project and that the policy was dictated by laws on the books as set out by the United States Congress. This meant: The acquisition of land or property was on the basis of negotiated purchase. The Government hoped every possible effort would be made to reach agreement on prices to avoid condemnation proceedings.

Then came the question: What is the appraisal procedure? The answer sounded reasonable: No individual's land or property could be taken without just compensation at a fair market value. And anyone would have the right to carry his case to the Federal Courts if he weren't satisfied with the Government's offer after negotiation.

Many people were interested in moving their homes to nearby communities. They wanted to know how to proceed: First, the Government would acquire the house. Then the owner could buy it back on the basis of salvage value. The difference in these values would represent some reimbursement for moving.

The discussion was long but peaceful. I came home, realizing as everyone else did, the hard months ahead—just how hard depended on the agreement of the people and Government on the definition of "just compensation."

Present for the meeting that night were many members of the press and a number of photographers. Immediately after the announcement of the H-Bomb's location, they couldn't get to Ellenton fast enough. We expected publicity—there was no way to avoid it—but not the kind they gave us.

Tempers flared when the people discovered photographers taking pictures of run-down houses. This was the way they'd depict Ellenton. Certainly the town had its share of poor people who lived in dilapidated places like any other town or city, but it also had decent homes and some beautiful ones. Why hadn't they photographed these, too? And the papers were full of what we didn't say to reporters more than what we really did tell them. They ignored the fact we were human beings who had intense pride and feelings—they wrote to entertain the public.

However, everyone was grateful for the reporters and photographers who did portray Ellenton correctly. That was the way the people wished it.

How glad I was for Saturday. Under normal conditions teaching is hard; but with upset children and a disturbed teacher, the atmosphere wasn't conducive for learning. I longed to obliterate the whole catastrophe, sleep soundly once more, and think of something pleasant.

Since Christmas was just a little more than three weeks off, I should make some plans for the holidays. But as hard as I tried, I couldn't muster up the Christmas spirit—no one else could either—instead, the horrible nightmare persisted.

Courtesy of the United States Atomic Energy Commission

A scene of the "Mouth of the Creek" that flows into the Savannah River.

Courtesy of U. S. Atomic Energy Commission

One of many freight trains coming in daily. This picture was taken on the day of the announcement.

Courtesy of Atomic Energy Commission

One of several clubhouses in the vicinity. Leigh Banana Case Company owned this one.

The front and side view of the author's home.

⟶ white, elite

The flower bordered walk that paralleled the house.

The huge Indica Azalea.

The gazing globe—an old millstone served for a base.

The other entrance through the arbor that led to the spacious lawn.

Courtesy of the U. S. Atomic Energy Commission

Reading from (right to left) the homes of Mrs. C. J. Ashley; Mrs. Elmo Ashley; and the Cassels' ancestral home.

Courtesy of the U. S. Atomic Energy Commission

Stately oaks such as this one sheltered many of the homes.

Courtesy of the U. S. Atomic Energy Commission

The U. S. Post Office building was formerly the Bank of Western Carolina. The Old Bonner House: The family originally used the small, third-story addition for worship. The Bonners were Ellenton's only Catholics.

[25]

Chapter II

A CHECKERED SUNDAY

It was Sunday, December 3. When I awoke that morning after a night of deep sleep, I felt refreshed and relaxed. I didn't remember immediately the unhappy experiences of the past week. But it didn't take Stark Reality long to sneak from his hiding place in the back of my mind and thrust himself into my presence to remind me. . . .

Propped up in bed on my elbow with my face cupped in my hand, I peeped through the half-opened shutters of the venetian blind to check on the weather. The partial view of our chocolate-colored lawn—stiff-looking from the extreme cold the week before—and the gray overcast sky showing itself above the shrubbery, presented a cold, bleak picture. "What weather!" I moaned. Dropping back on my pillow, I turned my eyes from the dreary scene; it accentuated my depressed feelings.

Suddenly I remembered how homesick I was the first few weeks at college when I woke up in the mornings, but it would dissipate like an early morning fog as soon as I got up and busied myself. So I sprang from bed hoping for the same results: I soon discovered that chasing away college-blues wasn't comparable to my present situation. And, if I could have visualized the diversity of events I'd experience that day, which caused me to run the gamut of emotions, I'm positive I'd have jumped back into bed and hibernated until Monday morning.

My checkered experiences began in the early afternoon at the church where I'd gone to practice the organ for evening services. The serene atmosphere of the sanctuary and the inspiring music served as a therapy. I could sense my built-up tension of the past week vanishing like a bird disappearing into the sky. I was normal again.

This healthy feeling lasted until I opened the church door to leave. Lively voices attracted my attention. I stopped dead; the scene offended my sensitive nature. A gay middle-aged couple, bubbling over with repartee, were taking pictures of our doomed church. I felt hot blood rush to my face. Then anger seized me. Trembling violently, I braced myself against the closed door. My voice seemed far away when I heard myself say, "How can you feel so indifferent and happy over our calamity? If it weren't the church . . ." Even though tears blurred my sight, I saw two silent and discomposed people quickly drive away.

Stumbling back into the church, I slumped on the back pew. I couldn't think; my mind was like a whirlwind. It was well over a half-hour before I regained calmness enough to rationalize the scene for which I'd been responsible. The aftermath of my indignation was one of disgust—disgust for allowing myself to display such resentment and for feeling sorry for myself. Those people had a right to take pictures and feel lighthearted. My unreasonable action shocked me. Determined never to let this happen again, I marched out like a winner in a contest.

Again, I was startled; something had happened! As far as I could see, cars almost bumper to bumper were milling around like ants. My heartbeat slowed down after I realized curiosity seekers had come to scrutinize the little town destined to die. "What better entertainment could they want on a cold, gray Sunday afternoon?" I asked in sarcasm, forgetting I was my only audience.

Ellenton had never before had a traffic jam. This was something new. Heretofore, if anyone wanted to turn around in the middle of the road, no one was inconvenienced. Now I couldn't even back my car from its parking place. Finally, one considerate driver held up the long line for me to join what looked like a funeral procession with cars crawling at a snail's pace. Exasperated, I was still grumbling about what a nuisance those out-of-town sight-seers were when I slipped into our driveway. Luckily I was on that side of the road.

Dashing into the house and on upstairs to my bedroom, I walked to the window and looked down on a continuous line of cars coming and going. One couldn't even cross the street— another new situation for Ellenton. I also noticed some people craning their necks to see beyond our tall shrubbery. In my mind I could hear exclamations of pity over destroying what must be a beautiful garden. How humiliating! I thought. By now my eyes had become so saturated with cars that the one in front of our home meant nothing more to me than the popular definition of a weed among flower-lovers—a plant out of place—except this time, it was a car.

While I was at the church, Mamie, weary of the pall that hung over the town, crawled on her favorite sofa and went to sleep. She'd had no desire to visit the garden lately; her poignant grief had kept her away. But when she woke up, the urge to see it overpowered her. As she strolled toward the front, the stream of passing cars surprised her; but the one parked in front of our house caught her attention immediately. In Ellenton a car parked outside your door meant company. Not recognizing anyone, she presumed the people were my friends because a Newberry, South Carolina, sticker was on the windshield, and she knew I had friends there. With no doubt in her mind, Mamie walked quickly to the car and introduced herself. Although their names weren't familiar when they returned the introduction, she suspected nothing; they were my friends and that was reason enough to extend them a cordial invitation to come in.

"Really we don't have time this afternoon," one lady said, "We just rode over . . ."

"Of course, it was so thoughtful of you. Louise will appreciate your coming."

When they attempted another excuse, Mamie protested, "You must take a few minutes and have a coke; by that time Louise will be here. She'll be so disappointed if she misses you."

As soon as Mamie heard me come in, she stepped into the hall and called, "Come down, Louise, some friends are here."

Mamie's voice broke my line of thought. I now remembered the car. Hastily I dabbed some powder on my face, rearranged an out-of-place wave in my hair, and under a mask of smiles, hurried down.

I could hear lively talking and laughter—sounds that had been absent from our home for almost a week. I couldn't imagine who the friends were, for I didn't recognize anyone's voice but Mamie's. My curiosity drew me on like a magnet. When I walked in, I didn't recognize a face. The guests turned their eyes toward the door as I entered, and I smiled around the room and introduced myself. Naturally, I wanted to give my sister's friends a warm welcome. "How wonderful," I said, "to come see Mamie. I'm so glad I came in time to meet you."

After I'd made that remark, I noticed a peculiar expression on Mamie's face, and a quietness crept over her. Suddenly, she reversed her behavior and became delightfully lively. She began relieving the guests of empty glasses and making herself the cynosure of the group. Knowing her as I did, I caught the meaning—she didn't mean for me to have any further conversation with *our* friends. But her inexplicable behavior—minutes before an enigma—cleared up like a summer sky after a storm.

Another emotion began bubbling in me. I dared not look at Mamie, nor she at me, for she was experiencing it, too. How glad I was when the guests rose to go. Gathering around Mamie, they lavished appreciation of her hospitality. Then turning to me, they expressed their delight in meeting me. As soon as they had driven off, our eyes met, and a spontaneous outburst of laughter shook us. Between convulsions, I managed to say, "Thanks . . . for your kindness . . . to my unknown . . . friends."

"Oh well," Mamie replied, trying to repress another fit of laughter, "it didn't hurt . . . to be nice to them."

Mamie's new friends proved their sincerity and appreciation of her hospitality. Like seed blown by the wind, they spread far and wide the news that the most hospitable person they'd ever met lived in Ellenton, the doomed town.

How grateful we were that this amusing experience had happened on the grayest of days and in the beginning of our hardships. For the past week we'd forgotten we ever had a sense of humor—an inherited trait our family had and always enjoyed. But now, we realized we had a powerful resource to rely upon when our topsy-turvy world closed in too fast upon us. And from time to time our sense of humor continued to relieve us of deep emotional feelings that otherwise would have brought us much stress and strain. We can yet laugh about the difficult experiences rather than remember the unhappy ones.

Once more I returned to my room to enjoy its privacy from sympathizers, sight-seers, newsmongers, and rubbernecks. Little did I realize that our town, even then, was beginning a metamorphosis. But unlike that of an ugly caterpillar emerging from its chrysalis into a beautiful butterfly, Ellenton would revert gradually from a beloved town where homes had once stood contentedly, into a devastated area of crumbling brick pillars and dug up gardens.

All at once darkness like a dust cloud filled my room. One look out the window told the story: The pale-gray canopy that had stretched itself smoothly over the heavens all day—and over our spirits, too— was now in dense dark-gray layers extending around and above the horizon. The elements seemed ready to burst into fury any minute; I'd hardly thought of it, when torrents of rain pelted the earth.

[31]

From the window I watched cars creeping toward the highway with their headlights on to prevent accidents. Gust after gust of strong winds picked up rain drops and sprayed cars, making the occupants look like outlined shadows. Whether the motorists could see or not, they had to keep moving. One stop would have begun a chain reaction of a front and back bumper collision. The only course to take was follow the leader. I could feel the weather getting colder; I closed the blinds and decided to dress for church.

Ellenton was proud of its churches—Methodist, Christian, and Baptist. All had modern sanctuaries, educational facilities, and pastoriums; and each enjoyed an almost full-time ministry by sharing its pastor with another church in a nearby community. By alternating, there was either a morning or an evening worship service. That night the Baptist Church would have its first service after the H-Bomb announcement. I feared the stormy weather would keep many people home, but I was mistaken. Regardless of the cold and continuing downpour of rain, the church's seating capacity of almost four hundred had to stretch itself to accommodate even more. This was evidence that the people felt the need of spiritual strength as well as physical endurance for tempestuous days ahead.

As the Reverend Robert D. Parkinson looked at his bewildered congregation that stormy, cold night, he felt assured he had selected the appropriate message to comfort his people. He based his subject, "When the Brook Dried Up," on I Kings 17:7. "And it came to pass . . . that the brook dried up . . ."

The Biblical background was during the time wicked King Ahab and his even more wicked, domineering wife, Jezebel, ruled over Israel. When Jezebel dared to destroy God's prophets and introduce Baal worship, God raised up Elijah to lead Israel from spiritual darkness into light again. One day this dramatic prophet boldly walked into the palace and announced to King

Ahab: "As the Lord God of Israel liveth . . . there shall not be dew nor rain these years, but according to my word" (I Kings 17:1).

During the three years of drought, God hid Elijah by the brook Cherith and supernaturally cared for him. Elijah probably would have stayed there all his life, but God had more and greater plans for him. So God allowed the brook to dry up. If Elijah had stayed, there would not have been that glorious day on Mt. Carmel when he prayed down fire and brought a nation back to God. Nor would there have been the many miracles he performed to abolish physical hunger and grief.

In detail, Mr. Parkinson gave other examples of Biblical and twentieth century men whose brooks God had allowed to dry up so their works would reach a higher plane.

In conclusion he said: "Today we are too close to the forest to see the trees. All that we see now are ugly trunks and underbrush; but as time goes on and we get farther away, we will be able to look up and view the forest in all its verdant glory.

"If ever a brook dried up for any people, it has dried up for us. It looks like a tragedy to us now because we do not realize what God has in store for us in the days ahead. Therefore, let us not be bitter; for we *know* that all things will work together for our good. Rather let us submit as long as we cannot do anything, for we know that this could not have happened to us unless it were in the divine plan of Almighty God.

"Instead of harboring hatred and bitterness for those who are going to give the orders, let us 'Render unto Caesar the things that are Caesar's, and to God, the things that are God's' and say, 'Lord, thy will be done.' "

Silently the congregation left the church. We'd found the solace for which we came—at least for the present.

Chapter III

AN UNHEEDED CHRISTMAS

Since Christmas was about three weeks off, the Ellenton people dared to hope reporters and photographers would take a vacation and give the town one, too. In fact, a permanent absence would have suited even more. The news media had combed the community clean for stories and pictures; surely, there was no reason for them to stay. But they did, and others continued to come. Disgusted and annoyed by so much publicity, everyone resorted to dodging them, and apparently derived a retributive enjoyment in playing hide-and-seek.

Naturally it was too early for the people to realize the significance of the H-Bomb project and its future ramifications. Besides, they were so disturbed and confused over their small world, nothing else mattered. But as the progress of this enormous plant unfolded before their eyes, they realized the impact it would have on the ever-shrinking world. This was a history-making epoch, the Atomic Age—the greatest the world had ever known—and Ellenton was a hotbed for news. Whether folk liked it or not, the news media had come to stay. Like a communicable, sporadic disease, they appeared almost anywhere at any time.

During the first few weeks after the Government had announced its plans, teaching became increasingly more difficult. My sixth-graders were mature enough to react to the shock of losing their homes and town, the same as adults—to a lesser degree, though. Moreover, they sensed their parents' problems, and this awareness had settled my once lively class into a listless, sober-minded group. This was the first time they'd ever deviated from their usual pattern of behavior at Christmas—effervescing like water charged with carbon dioxide. As much as I'd always dreaded this daily crescendo of liveliness preceding the holidays, I preferred it to my unhappy pupils. I became so sympathetic that I masked my true feelings to transform theirs from seriousness to happiness.

Trying hard one morning to hold the children's attention as I explained an arithmetic problem at the blackboard, I noticed they were staring in the direction of the door. Turning, I followed their gaze; standing in the door was a stranger.

"I'm sorry," I said, "I didn't hear your knock."

"N-no," he replied, not at all abashed, "I just slipped in."

Immediately I knew why he was there; a stubborn muteness overwhelmed me. So, I stood silently looking at the stranger and made no move to welcome him. Neither did the children stir; they, too, just stared and waited. No doubt he sensed he wasn't wanted. But the awkward silence didn't discourage him, rather he was busy looking around the room—deciding, I suppose, from what angle he'd take a picture. Then calmly and politely he stated: "I'd like to take a picture of you and your class at work."

Knowing the principal was away for the morning and I was safe from intrusion, hypocritically I replied, "Sorry." Then truthfully I explained, "The principal will have to give you permission."

Secretly rejoicing over winning my point, I returned to my work as the photographer rushed out to find the principal. The children expressed no disappointment over my decision; the thrill of having their pictures made had lost its attraction. Now it was a bore. The incident temporarily lifted my spirits. At recess I enjoyed the "good-for-you" admiration of the teachers. Altogether the occurrences of the morning had pleased me.

In about an hour there was a loud rap on the door. Before I could answer it, in stepped the photographer with his paraphernalia and handed me a note. My eyes widened when I rec-

By permission of United Press Association

Louise Cassels and her sixth grade class. The picture that touched the heart of the nation.

ognized the principal's signature. Where had he found him? Reluctantly, I had to consent. Although this stranger had won through perseverance, his courteous and understanding manner melted my strong resentment of him. After completing his assignment, he turned to me and asked in a concerned manner, "How do you and others feel about sacrificing your town?"

"We're heartsick at being displaced; but if it's for the good of the country, we'll co-operate 100 per cent."

During December and January the picture appeared in many newspapers and school pamphlets throughout the United States with my reply as a caption. And to my surprise, the picture was splendid—despite the fact I wasn't photogenic. What was even more amazing, the effects of the picture were far-reaching. For almost two months letters poured in. I was so entertained by my fan mail I felt like a national figure.

Teachers and compassionate people bombarded me with sympathy letters that acted like an opiate to my injured pride. I soon discovered, though, that sympathy was the wrong treatment for me; it brought on self-pity. Like measles, I could feel myself breaking out with it.

But the letter that lifted my morale was one from an elderly lady in North Carolina. She turned her concern into action when she invited me to live with her in her two-story home and use part of it for a private school. Then, after her death, she'd make me heir to all her property. Her letter reflected the sincerity of the offer by including an invitation to visit her with all expenses paid so I could make my own decision. Even though it wasn't advantageous for my profession or for me to accept her kindness, I felt flattered and grateful.

Sprinkled among the mountain of sympathetic letters were always some from money-makers. Whatever they had to sell was "the finest of its kind." I wondered why they'd want to part with such valuable property or possessions. A letter from Oregon was typical: An air-conditioned supermarket ideally situated with all modern equipment was for sale, and for living conveniences, an upstairs apartment. "It's an exceptional bargain for the price," he wrote. I'm positive from the fantastic amount he asked, he had no doubt that the Ellenton people had had a windfall at the Government's expense.

Perhaps the most amusing offer came from Missouri: Pocket-size pictures, like politicians hand out to voters, fluttered to the floor from a bulky letter I was opening.

"Look at that hog," I chuckled, pushing the picture toward Mamie with my foot. "It's king-size, large enough to ride."

"You mean to whet one's appetite for a home-cured ham."

"Both." I laughed.

The owner wanted to sell a large fertile farm for raising corn and livestock. To impress me with the results of his labor, he'd sent the pictures. I was impressed but not the way he intended: I wasn't a character in a fairy tale book that a magic wand could turn an elementary teacher into a successful farmer overnight. I was merely a human being lost in a maze for the present; eventually I'd work myself out into a sensible world again. Nevertheless, I was grateful for the humorous suggestions for my future. At least they added zest to what would have been a passive Christmas.

By now the entire nation was aware of Ellenton's predicament —it was the top news of the year. Not even for a day were the people allowed to forget their disaster. The news media shouted it through the papers and over the radio. Moreover, many South Carolina towns sent official committees to invite the community to become part of them. Pensacola, Florida, offered a unique solution: It would help rebuild the town intact on a tract of land near the city. We'd have to change our name though, for Florida already had a small town named Ellenton. This unusual hospitality impressed us. It was like friends opening their homes to the homeless. No one could forget that.

Ultimately though, everyone had to base his important decision of relocation on existing circumstances. Certain requisites would be necessary for some businesses, such as Leigh Banana Case Company—Ellenton's only industry—and the Chevrolet dealership. Then many would have to locate either in an unincorporated town or face keen competition in a larger place: The funeral home, the dry cleaners, the drugstore, and the depository faced this fate. And the telephone system—Ellenton had enjoyed the dial system years before larger towns had used it—faced a similar decision.

Farmers had their difficulties, too, especially those who did extensive, diversified farming. They realized a replacement of their land and farm labor would be almost impossible. They'd either have to retire much earlier than they had anticipated or they'd have to decrease their farming activities.

To add to their mounting problems, planting another year's crop was contingent on when the Government would acquire their property. This disturbing delay affected both farmers and labor. The situation brought on a restlessness that was hard to cope with. So Christmas of all seasons, symbolic of peace and joy, produced only frustration and hardship.

I missed the cheerfulness of the homes: Absent were the colored Christmas lights that glowed from window sills, and glimpses of Christmas trees in the background winking their multicolored lights as though flirting with passers-by. Conspicuously absent, too, were Christmas wreaths on front doors and outdoor decorations on symmetrical cedars, tapering toward the sky and studded artistically from top to ground with lights.

Despite conditions though, there were some reminders of Christmas: School children, whose sensitivity I thought had sunk to zero, released their pent-up emotions and antagonistic feelings by shooting firecrackers at full blast. The loud noises sounded like a daily battle waging in the vicinity. Judging by this, I should have normal children to teach hereafter, that is, if I survived my normalcy during those daily attacks.

Then stouthearted parents, determined their children shouldn't return to college with the memory of a drab holiday as their last in Ellenton, struggled through the celebration of Christmas. Their lighted trees and outside decorations served as a beacon here and there to brighten a dying town.

At least I was thankful for church services. There only, could I find the embodiment of the real Christmas spirit and enjoy respite from the turbulent activities of the week. To listen to the singing of familiar carols and to hear the old, old story of Jesus' birth—always miraculously new—gave me a sense of peace I couldn't describe. That part of my life man couldn't disturb or buy. It was intact. Otherwise, Christmas came and went unheeded.

Chapter IV

PERPLEXING TIMES

Early in January, 1951, signs for beginning construction of the H-Bomb plant appeared. Massive machinery on flat railroad cars, left on a spur track for unloading, evinced the town a construction crew would soon follow. Ironically, this very railroad—built almost ninety years ago—had been the incentive for the birth of Ellenton. Now it had turned traitor and become allied to the Government: It was transporting equipment that would change a peaceful, typical southern town of warmhearted folk to a mammoth plant for producing materials that could destroy the world.

At this time no one's imagination could stretch itself sufficiently—not even if it were elastic—to visualize the amount of various materials the Government would need for construction. These few cars were only forerunners for the 126,000 carloads to follow. And, if they'd been placed in a single giant train, it would have reached from Atlanta, Georgia, to the Pennsylvania Railroad Station in New York City.

Regardless of how everyone had hoped to keep Ellenton intact—at least for a few months longer—it proved as futile as holding a dying man's hand to prevent Death from snatching him away. It was evident now our town would never enjoy normalcy again; every week brought drastic changes: Construction crews began arriving by the thousands in trailers with their families. (By June 8,000 had come. The number increased continuously until it reached its peak of 38,580 on September 30, 1952.) Not only did they scatter over our community, adding to the existing hodgepodge effect that kept Ellenton from being an attractive town, but also settled in enormous trailer courts over Aiken and Barnwell counties.

With this rapid influx of people, business flourished and increased steadily every week. Never had Ellenton experienced such a boom—a false prosperity I called it.

These migratory people also swelled the congregations of the churches. Coming from every section of the United States, and having lived in many different parts of it, naturally they were different from the local people. Notwithstanding these diversities, devout people were found among them and seemed happy to have a church home for a short time.

No doubt though, the school was more affected in this transitional stage than any of the other organizations: With the enrollment steadily increasing, the school building was soon filled. To house the overflow the trustees asked for the use of every available building in town for educational facilities, e v e n churches.

Furthermore, teachers lived and taught under *extreme tension:* Keeping down friction between the highly sensitive trailer children and the local ones created a task within itself. The least incident could stir up indignation and erupt into an explosion of wrath. So our goal of holding our beloved town intact as long as possible was lost in the maze of existing problems.

The Government was moving fast now in acquiring areas around Ellenton needed for construction, which would begin on February 1. Appraisers were already on the job, and property owners were nervously waiting to hear the results of these first negotiations: They'd indicate what we might expect in future transactions. The suspense was tantamount to the time when we could hardly wait to find out what was "coming to Ellenton." So the people could only hope they'd receive just compensation for their property.

Each afternoon I hurried home from school hoping to hear encouraging news from the negotiations. The minute I'd entered the house I'd hunt for Mamie. This afternoon I found her in the kitchen sitting at a table arranging camellias. She anticipated my question before I could ask. "No news yet," she said, looking up from her flower arrangement.

"Company coming?" I asked, walking toward the table.

"No. I'm going to enjoy these. There's no use to leave them for the cold to kill."

"They're beautiful," I said, picking up a lovely variegated one to scrutinize it more closely. How we'll miss them, I thought. I knew Mamie was thinking the same thing; but neither said it.

Unexpectedly, Arthur strode into the kitchen looking relieved for the first time in weeks. "I ran in to tell you Jimmy Stone got his check from the Government a few minutes ago, and he's satisfied with what he received for his house and farm."

While Arthur was talking one of Mamie's hands gripped the flower container, the other held a camellia in air ready to place in the arrangement. Her pose looked as though she'd purposely frozen in that p o s i t i o n for a pantomime. "Whoopee!" she shouted and jabbed the camellia in the first vacant spot she saw.

"Wonderful!" I said, clapping my hands.

Arthur held up his hand like a policeman stopping traffic. "Let's *hope* it'll continue this way."

Like a running fire the good news spread over town. When the radio announced it that evening, the report was old to Ellentonians. Despite the circuitous route, the grapevine system had proved itself speedier than the radio or newspaper medium. This time photographers and reporters didn't get ahead. But the picture of a Government agent handing a check to a smiling farmer for his property, along with a reporter's story, was already headed for the front pages of many newspapers next morning.

After the second week of satisfactory negotiations the people relaxed; they expected later transactions to follow the same pattern. Somehow though I had misgivings about such smooth sailing. So, I wasn't surprised when I heard other appraisers had replaced the first. Evidently the Government thought negotiations had become too satisfactory.

Indignant property owners resented the Federal Government's attitude. It was one thing to give up one's inheritance for a needed cause when compensated well, but another thing to give it up and have to sell for a pittance. The people became defiant. "Why," they complained to one another, "should the Government stint on its own citizens, leaving us in worse financial condition than before, and at the same time pour money into foreign countries that don't appreciate it?" This feeling mushroomed until it terminated into a hotly contested war (lasting about two years) with battles waging in and out the court room. No jury could honestly go against the people; the verdict was always for them. And, in cases settled out of court the Government compensated sufficiently to lessen tension.

In other ways, too, property-owners had little consideration shown them when the Government needed certain areas: Arthur, along with others, was caught in that predicament. Two weeks before the announcement of the H-Bomb's coming, he'd gone to Wisconsin and bought a good many cows to replenish his stock. Unfortunately his dairy and pastures, extending to the river, lay in the territory needed immediately. It was impossible for Arthur to sell all his cows and dairy equipment on such short notice without considerable loss. Everyday he was somewhere hunting a buyer. Regardless of the situation though, the Government took down pasture fences and cows roamed everywhere.

I was leaving for school one morning when the phone delayed me. "Hello," I answered quickly.

"I wish to speak to Mr. Foreman."

"Sorry, but he isn't here."

"Where can I find him?"

"I've no idea. He left early this morning."

"But I *must* get in touch with him," the emphatic voice said.

Realizing something had gone wrong, I asked, "Is your business with him urgent?"

"I should say so. His cows are on the railroad track, and the train can't pass. He *must* get them off immediately."

His demanding voice exasperated me, for I knew the untold trouble Arthur had had trying to protect his cows until he could sell them for at least a fair price. So, I asked a question to remind the annoyed man of the trouble the Government had caused. "Who took the fences down?"

"The Government *had* to."

"Then the Government will *have* to get the cows off the track."

Not giving the man time to reply, I excused myself by explaining I was on my way to school and would have to leave the phone. After running by Mamie's room to inform her of the conversation, I hurried on.

That afternoon Mamie and I rode to the dairy; everything was in order. Evidently the Government had had to take my advice. "Before we go home let's ride over some other areas to see what's going on," Mamie said, closing the half-opened car window.

"Suits me fine," I said, turning the car around and heading toward the highway.

For the next hour the alpha of a new era and the omega of Ellenton stretched out before us: Fields recently white with cotton or green with corn presented strange scenes. Giant pipes large enough for an adult to walk through lay in deep excavations headed toward the Savannah River. In other areas men swarmed around like bees, laying foundations for buildings. Then, as if we'd driven from an industrial site into a farming community, we saw farmers clearing their fields for one more year of planting.

Puzzled over passing so many fenced-in plots of different sizes, we parked the car and walked over a field to satisfy our curiosity. As we neared the mysterious spectacle, a tombstone

Courtesy of the United States Atomic Energy Commission

These giant pipes heading toward the Savannah River would provide millions of gallons of water for operating the plant.

darkened with age barely leveled the railing. "A cemetery!" I exclaimed. "Why couldn't we have guessed that?"

Often fences enclosed unmarked graves; otherwise we wouldn't have known it was a cemetery. "I had no idea there were so many small ones around Ellenton," Mamie said, as we walked back to the car.

"Neither did I. And have you noticed the precautions the Government has taken to protect them?"

"Yes. You know the Government is responsible to every family for its dead. Not only will it have to move those bodies but also provide a cemetery for them."

"I know," I said. We'd reached the car, but we continued standing as we talked.

"I prefer to move our dead and buy a lot wherever we live. The Government can pay us for the vacated cemetery and move the monuments." Mamie paused and looked at me to study my response. Then she continued, "I hope you feel the same way?"

"I do, and I'm glad we've settled that question."

On our way back as we were passing the funeral home, Mamie exclaimed, "Stop! There's a fence around something here."

I backed to see what it was. The Government had built a neat little railing around a tombstone that the funeral director had used for advertising.

"Let's go home; I need the phone," I said, starting the motor. "The grapevine must circulate this news so everyone can see that sight before sundown. It will do their morale good."

Next morning on my way to school, I thought about the experiences of yesterday . . . fences . . . fences . . . fences. How ridiculous! The Government had built them to protect the dead and torn down the ones needed to protect the living.

The Government's fast pace of taking over our easy-going town reminded me of a toboggan ride I once had: After starting, there was no stopping, and I gained such momentum on the way down that I spun around several times after I'd reached the bottom. The Ellenton people had reached the bottom, but they were still spinning. That's why everyone was busy renovating his home—not for a festive occasion but for the appraisal. They figured the purchasing price would be higher if the house looked good.

Those with gardens were equally concerned. To them they were priceless possessions and part of their life. Money couldn't pay for the many hours of patience, tender care, and love it had taken to grow them. But gardeners realized the Government viewed gardens as merely another piece of property. With that cold fact ever before them, they paid reliable nurseries to evaluate their gardens to serve as a check on the Government's offer.

In a few weeks Ellenton had taken on a gala appearance. Never before had homes and gardens greeted spring in such attractive regalia. The overall picture gave me a fleeting pride but a sinking heart; all too soon a void would replace the scene. It reminded me of a well-groomed corpse lying in state for friends and relatives to admire before taking the body to its last resting place.

From then on the town waited . . . . Housekeepers kept spotless homes and stayed close; gardeners weeded, trimmed, and mowed lawns daily. But the dread of appraisals hung over the people like an approaching operation.

Their emotional response swung like a pendulum between dejection and elation: Every day was one less for the old, comfortable life; yet, one day nearer freedom from the talons of the Government.

Naturally during this period, families were giving more thought to their future plans—certainly Arthur was.

"Extensive farming is out of the question," he said. "I think I'll dabble in real estate for a while." Then with a twinkle in his eyes, "Or retire to fish."

Actually, we delayed our plans until Fielding, Mamies and Arthur's unmarried son just out of college, knew where he could relocate his Chevrolet dealership. Headquarters had to make the decision.

Unexpectdly the green light flashed on and in a day's time our plans crystalized. The Chevrolet Company permitted Fielding to locate eight miles south of Aiken, South Carolina, on the road to the H-Bomb plant where a nameless, new town was mushrooming. Without any discussion we knew immediately we'd live in Aiken. The decision pleased us; for we already had friends there.

Chapter V

TRYING TO GET A HOME

Next day Mamie and I drove to Aiken, twenty-seven miles north of Ellenton, to hunt for either a house or a lot. But the influx of AEC and du Pont people had left it practically devoid of both. The few still available didn't fit our needs.

"Houses and lots are as scarce in Aiken as good people were in Sodom and Gomorrah when God destroyed them," I said, on the way home.

"We'll keep trying," Mamie replied, but I detected disappointment in her voice.

Fortunately about two weeks later, we found a symmetrical, wooded area of pines just out the city limits for sale. The front faced famous old Whiskey Road (a historical name derived from its use in carrying whiskey and rum from the Atlantic Coast to the North). In developing this property, roads were named in conformity with it. Brandy, which bisected the area, ran perpendicular to Whiskey; Gin and Sherry intersected Brandy at different points to form three blocks of beautiful lots. Now old Whiskey Road had three alcoholic neighbors.

"Mercy me," I said, shaking my head, "how'll we ever explain to our friends that living on the corner of Whiskey and Brandy is decent and beautiful?"

No sooner would we solve one knotty problem than another would face us. It reminded me of people in queue: When one moved on another took his place. We now owned a beautiful lot but had no architect. Realizing the demand for them in such a widespread building program, we began our safari next day. For over a week we hunted and begged relentlessly; but the pattern of every visit varied only in the manner each expressed his regrets. "So sorry . . . just impossible . . . deluged . . . wish I could, but . . ." However, the need of a home prodded us on.

One night after a disheartening all-day hunt, our cousin, Mildred, who lived in Augusta and had joined the search party, telephoned. Her voice was buoyant. "I've found one!"

"Eureka," I shouted.

Mamie standing by grabbed the phone to hear the news first-hand. "Where *did* you find him?"

I dashed upstairs to get on the other phone just in time to hear Mildred say, "Mr. Davis decided to leave the firm he was with to open his own. I've an engagement for you tomorrow at three."

The news electrified us. We were like two excited children who couldn't wait for tomorrow to play with a new toy. Plans for our new home began whirling around in our minds, making sleep impossible. So in the quiet of a warm spring night, a new home was born in our imagination. Would that the actual house could have materialized as quickly as the dream!

The public usually referred to the people who'd have to move as displaced persons or "D.P.'s." I *hated* the term. But as I walked out the architect's office the next afternoon, I shed that nomenclature forever. We were no longer homeless evacuees. We now owned a lot, and soon we'd have a new home on it with a front and back yard. This was the anchor I needed to restore my confidence in belonging once more to the real world.

Planning our new home in comparison to the many difficult problems that had confronted us was as refreshing as a cool breeze after a long hot spell.

"I'm so pleased with the plans," I said to Mamie, after one of our many consultations with the architect.

"So am I. It takes some of the sting out of leaving the home we've lived in and loved all our life."

On a warm morning about the middle of June our garden, as if overnight, had entered another cycle of beauty. Spring had just finished its colorful display of azaleas and dogwoods; and purple wisteria climbing tree trunks or falling gracefully from arbors had added its beauty along with showy bulbs and other spring flowers. Now the entire scene had changed to bushes, trees, and vines dressed in fresh, tender green leaves with stretches of smooth, clean-shaven lawns reaching out from them.

"Nature is wonderful," I said. "Every season has its individual beauty; before we tire of one, we have another."

"The summer garden is so restful to the eye and gives a feeling of coolness," Mamie replied. We were sitting in the solarium enjoying this beauty when the door bell rang.

Automatically we looked at each other. "Appraisers!" I exclaimed. We jumped to our feet so fast our chairs were still rocking when we left.

I knew my guess was right the instant I saw a strange, middle-aged man, slightly tall with graying hair standing at the door. Mamie realized it, too; for I saw a flood of resentment in her face.

"I'm Mr. Wight, a horticulturist, from the University of Georgia. I've come to appraise your garden."

I'm not sure if Mamie and I ever introduced ourselves. But Mamie's exacting voice steadied me somewhat, for inwardly I was trembling violently. "All right, sir; we're ready. But I should warn you, we know the value of our garden. Fruitland Nursery has appraised it, and I have the papers. If it's not appraised correctly, *you* and the *Government* will hear from us."

Evidently Mamie's strong tone intimidated the poor man. Next day he asked for the private appraisal. "I'll go by it," he said. Mamie gladly gave it to him.

By July house appraisals were in full swing. The people clung to their homes; yet, they realized relief would come only after the event was over. And the idea of not receiving just compensation for their property produced tension. No one enjoyed the thought of a legal fight with the mighty U. S. Government.

One day Mary, my teacher friend, had urgent business in Augusta. I drove her there. Not knowing the day the appraisers might come, she called her servant into the living room and instructed him what to do if the appraisers should come while she was away.

"Eddie, the first thing you do is to ask their names. If one is Mr. Bricker, *don't* let 'em in."

"*No ma'am*, he's de one you don' like."

"Right. Just tell 'em I'm not home and they'll have to come again."

"Well, Miss Mary, if neer one ain't Mr. Bricker, kin I let 'em in?" Eddie was staring at her wild-eyed.

"Yes. And give them those papers on my desk," she replied, pointing to them.

"Weezer," Mary said, turning to me, "that old Bricker appraised my farm so low I'm suing the Government. If I can help it, he's not appraising my home."

When we returned late that afternoon, Eddie ran to the car talking excitedly. "Deys been, Miss Mary!"

I turned off the engine and Mary didn't move. Eddie stood by the car and related the event. "I done jest what you tol' me. When I open the doo, I sez, 'is anyone of you name Mr. Bricker?' and when dey sez, 'no,' I let 'em in. Dey ain't been gone long."

"Thanks for taking me, Weezer. I'll let you know something as soon as I can." With that Mary hurried into the house.

Every day Mamie and I hoped the house appraisers would come, but it seemed they were always busy appraising the other person's home. Unexpectedly their delay precipitated a crisis in our progress. In about two weeks we'd have the house plans. But the contract for construction couldn't be let until the Government appraised and paid us for our home. We had no ready cash. We felt caged in like birds. And when we heard evacuation day would be on March 1, the news threw us into a tailspin. That gave us only six months in which to get a home finished. (Since the Government was ahead of schedule, the deadline was moved up from about July to March.) Even with smooth going it would be a close race; for the last half of the six months would be in the dead of winter.

So I decided I'd have to cash my U. S. Government bonds— just a few years from maturity—and Mamie would have to borrow. Her only collateral was "when the Government pays us." On these terms the bank loaned her money. The timing was perfect; plans and money came in simultaneously.

Contractors, like architects, were hard to find. The extensive building program in the Savannah River Area had devoured them like hungry men gobbling down food. After settling for the second best bidder—and thankful for him, despite our disappointment over not having the one we wanted—one more complication thwarted us before we could begin construction: A law prohibited us from building another home before the Government had paid us for the present one. So we had to build in Arthur's name and provide him with money. After the Government paid us, he'd deed the home to us. (This law, I discovered later, pertained only to entailed property.)

By October the framework of our two-storied house stood high among the tall, slender pine trees, too thick for growth except upward. And the warm, sunshiny fall days provided good building conditions to speed its completion. If only the weather would continue to favor us, we might evacuate on time.

On a Saturday afternoon about the middle of October, I was in the yard washing my car when I noticed four men walking through the driveway. Immediately I knew they were appraisers. A tinge of resentment passed over me for the moment, but Common Sense quickly advised me to turn my feelings into humor. "Look out, Gentlemen," I cried, pointing the hose toward them, "I've got you where I want you."

One of the four, a fat, stumpy, good-natured man held up his hands and shouted, "Wait, sprinkle the others! I'm a Baptist, they're Methodist and Presbyterians."

Our jesting created a friendly atmosphere that relieved any discomfiture that might have existed. Mamie, hearing us talking and laughing, hurried out. "Sounds like a circus out here," she said.

"It almost was," I replied.

One of the visitors said, "We were admiring your garden as we came in. What is the name of the bush that's perfumed the entire town with such a delightful odor?"

"Osmanthus fragrans, comonly known as tea olive," I said. "It's my favorite shrub. It blooms in the fall and the spring."

After a few minutes talk about flowers, one of the men introduced himself and the others. "I'm sure you know our mission. . . ."

"Yes," Mamie interrupted, we've been expecting you a long time."

Silently Mamie and I conducted the men to the house. "We'll be in the yard. Call us if you need us," I said, as we turned to leave.

"I'm going to finish washing my car," I said to Mamie. "Work'll steady my nerves and keep an hour from having a hundred twenty minutes instead of sixty. What'll you be doing?"

"My nerves need steadying, too. I'll be working in the garden."

The sun was a big red ball hanging low in the western sky when Mamie and I returned to the house; the appraisers had finished and were standing in the entrance hall. We dared not mention what was uppermost in our minds, that is, the price they'd appraised our home for. Nor did they give us any clues.

I was relieved it was finally over. Although deep in my heart, I knew our home had slipped from us on that beautiful October day.

"I hope the Government will move faster in making us an offer than it did in appraising the house," Mamie said.

Unfortunately, we soon found out that our ordeal with appraisers wasn't over. A week later another came, bringing his helper. Three weeks later two more showed up. We were mystified. I decided that getting appraised was like chain smoking—once you started there was no stopping. The only explanation Mamie and I could figure out was that the appraisers must have disagreed on the value of our home. What a predicament!

Chapter VI

THE EXODUS BEGINS

When the Government proclaimed March 1 as evacuation day, Ellenton entered into a chaotic state. Automatically the announcement affected the school: It would have to conclude the last three months of its term in Jackson, a village between Ellenton and Augusta, where a school building program was already in progress.

It also hastened the departure of families not moving to near-by towns. To enter their children in school by January 1 and to begin life anew, they left after Christmas Day. But most of the young married people had bought back their homes and business houses from the Government at salvage prices and engaged house-movers to move them before March 1, either to Jackson or to a mushrooming new town between Ellenton and Aiken which later was named New Ellenton.

It was a strange sight to see a familiar home jacked up on the chassis of a truck moving up the highway. Behind it followed a long string of cars at a funeral's pace. Finally the driver would find a wide place by the road to park and let the line of cars go by, only to accumulate another following when the truck reentered the highway.

In the meantime Ellenton began to look unique: Here and there stood homes fresh and clean in their new coats of paint, waiting to be moved while all around them were snaggletoothed spaces with front steps going nowhere and a maze of weeds growing in the place of a once-upon-a-time well-groomed garden.

My brother Mike, manager of Cassels' store,—more commonly known as the Long Store because of its length of 210 feet—began

Courtesy of the U. S. Atomic Energy Commission

Cassels Company, Inc., appropriately called "The Long Store," was older than many of Ellenton's citizens.

to liquidate the business in November. In this fifty-year-old general store, typical of small towns, one could buy just about anything from a toothpick to a mule's collar. The heating system was relatively simple: A large modern heater took care of the front, and a potbellied stove that glowed red on winter days heated the rear. This was the cynosure of the store and indeed of the town's life. Around it stood a circle of straight wooden chairs with stout cowhide bottoms and worn back legs—a result of the backward tilting position in which they were used. From early morning until late afternoon, male customers coming into the store would take time to "set a spell" in these chairs. They debated how to correct the evils of the world, the nation, and the state. Somehow I doubt there was much wisdom imparted around that hot stove, but judging from the laughter, there must have been a lot of wit, anyway.

At the back of the store was Mike's private office. Its furnishings consisted of a long leather couch, a large wooden rocker, and an old rolled-top desk strewn with papers and a telephone half hidden among them. From this desk, Mike ran the business most efficiently. He needed no better intercom than his deep, stentorian voice, calling first for one employee, then another. Occasionally he'd join the potbellied-stove crowd to add his humor and wit. In fact the store was so saturated with his personality that the two words, "Mike" and "Long Store," became synonymous.

Adjoining the front of the store on the left was a combination office and depository. (This depository was the first one in South Carolina. It came into existence by an act of the legislature after a chain of banks, called the Bank of Western Carolina, had failed.) Unlike the flavor of the store, it had every modern convenience. My eldest brother, Wallace, had managed this part of the business until his death, previous to the coming of the plant. The depository would now be transferred to Jackson.

In Cassels' famous country store, "The Long Store," residents of Ellenton are sitting around the pot-bellied stove discussing the Atomic Energy Project soon to come.

Mike arranged his desk neatly for the picture.

The State of South Carolina
EXECUTIVE DEPARTMENT

CHARTER
BY THE SECRETARY OF STATE

17544

WHEREAS,

H. M. Cassels, W. B. Cassels, S. M. Cassels, and
A. A. Foreman, all of Ellenton, S.C.

did on the **11th.** day of **April**, 1932,

signed by themselves, setting forth:

FIRST: That their names and residences are as above given.

SECOND: That the name of the proposed corporation is

ELLENTON CASH DEPOSITORY.

THIRD: That the principal place of business is

ELLENTON, S.C.

FOURTH: That the general nature of the business which it is proposed to do is **limited banking business as authorized under Act of the General Assembly approved April 7th. 1932, providing for "Cash Depositories"**

FIFTH: That the amount of the capital stock is **Twenty-five Hundred ($2,500.00)------- Dollars,** payable **in cash.**

SIXTH: That the number of shares into which the capital stock is divided is **twenty-five (25)** of the par value of **One Hundred ($100.00)------------ Dollars.**

SEVENTH: That, after due notice, a meeting of the subscribers was held on the **9th.** day of **April**, 1932, at which a majority of all stock in value being present in person or by proxy, the following were elected directors:

H.M.Cassels, S.M.Cassels, W.B.Cassels, and A. A. Foreman.

EIGHTH: That subsequently there was elected as President, **H. M. Cassels** as Vice-President, **A. A. Foreman**; as Secretary, **W.B.Cassels** as Treasurer, **W.B.Cassels.**

NINTH: That all requirements of Article 2, Chapter 153, Code of Laws of South Carolina, 1932, and all amendments thereto have been duly and fully complied with, 50 per cent. of the aggregate amount of the capital stock having been subscribed by bona fide subscribers, 20 per cent. of the capital stock subscribed having been paid to the Treasurer, and three days' public notice of the intention to file this Declaration with the Secretary of State having been given in **Journal & Review** a newspaper published in the County of **Aiken**

NOW, THEREFORE, I, W. P. BLACKWELL, Secretary of State, by virtue of the authority in me vested by the aforesaid Code and Acts amendatory thereto, do hereby certify that the said Company has been fully organized according to the laws of South Carolina, under the name and for the purposes indicated in their written declaration, and that they are fully authorized to commence business under their charter; and I do hereby direct that a copy of this certificate be filed and recorded in the office of the Register of Mesne Conveyance or Clerk of Court in each county where such Corporation shall have a business office.

GIVEN under my hand and the seal of the State, at Columbia. this **11th.** day of **April** in the year of our Lord on ethousand nine hundred and **thirty-two** and in the one hundred and fifty-**sixth** year of the Independence of the United States of America.

- W. P. BLACKWELL,
Secretary of State.

STATE OF SOUTH CAROLINA
EXECUTIVE DEPARTMENT

Pursuant to law the Capital Stock of the within Corporation has this day been increased to the sum of $75,000.00 — Seventy-five Thousand — — — Dollars, divided into Thirty-Seven (30,000) shares of the par value of $ 2.50 — Two - 50/100 Dollars each.

Given under my Hand and the Seal of the State at Columbia, this 20th day of November, 1963.
O. Frank Thornton
Secretary of State

STATE OF SOUTH CAROLINA
EXECUTIVE DEPARTMENT

Pursuant to law the Capital Stock of the within Corporation has this day been Increased to the sum of $50,000.00 Fifty Thousand — — — Dollars, divided into Ten Thousand (10,000) shares of the par value of $5.00 Five — — — dollars each.

Given under my Hand and the Seal of the State at Columbia, this 14th day of October A.D. 1957.
C. Frazier — —
Secretary of State

STATE OF SOUTH CAROLINA
EXECUTIVE DEPARTMENT

Pursuant to law the Capital Stock of the within Corporation has this day been Increased to sum of $62,500.00 Sixty-two Thousand and Five Hundred Dollars, divided into Two Thousand (500) shares of the par value of $5.00 — Five — Dollars each.

Given under my Hand and the Seal of the State at Columbia, this 26th day of February, 1963.
O. Frank Thornton
Secretary of State

STATE OF SOUTH CAROLINA
EXECUTIVE DEPARTMENT

Pursuant to law the Capital Stock of the within Corporation has this day been Increased to the sum of $150,000.00 One Hundred Fifty Thousand Dollars, divided into Sixty Thousand shares of the par value of $2.50 Two - 50/100 Dollars each.

Given under my Hand and the Seal of the State at Columbia, this 21 day of Dec. A.D. 1963.
Secretary of State

After terminating these institutions, there was nothing to hold Mike in Ellenton; by Christmas he was living in Aiken.

The usual gusto with which Ellentonians had always enjoyed Thanksgiving and Christmas was now out-of-the-question. Shortness of time demanded the people to spend the holidays very differently: They had to close out business affairs or depart for a new life. So at the best, it had to be only a family-day celebration.

During January and February each one in our family was living an occupied and separate life. Seldom were we together, even at meal time. Our faithful cook, Geraldine, kept house, and like the hub of a wheel held us together.

Fielding commuted to his re-established Chevrolet business, leaving early and returning late; the most we saw of him was on Sunday.

After Arthur had quit farming, he undertook the tremendous task of moving his tenants' houses to the new town between Ellenton and Aiken. Hiring house-movers and using some of his own labor, he filled the road with houses for weeks—even to the last day.

One of Arthur's helpers was a large, good-natured, very black-skinned Negro nicknamed "Snow," who habitually spent his weekends away. Returning late one Monday morning, "Snow" was shocked speechless to find his house missing from its foundation and well on its way to a new site.

Mamie had the responsibility of keeping up with the construction of our house. So she had to spend most of her time in Aiken.

Because teaching kept me in Ellenton, I inherited the job of sorting through a mountain of things accumulated over the years to decide which should be discarded before I began packing. Although the sight of some things I found in the attic evoked memories that clouded my eyes with tears, I'd get so interested in what had seemed so important for one generation and useless for another that I derived a peculiar enjoyment from it. It was like stepping back into the past for a moment. Often cardboard boxes surrounding me contained more things to save than to destroy. I knew I couldn't keep all those things; there'd be no place for them in the new house. So I'd hurriedly grab the "keep" boxes, rush to the back yard, and before I could have a change of heart, I'd toss them onto a bonfire. Sometimes the flames sprang so high, people would rush in from the street to help me put out the fire.

"Thanks," I'd say, "but I'm only burning the past."

One afternoon as I was clearing out Mother's pantry which she'd used for storing things that someone might conceivably use again, I found many useless but interesting antiques. There were stacks of old dishes, a fireless cooker, and a small crockery jar used for churning butter. A round wooden top with a hole in the center fitted the jar's mouth firmly. Through the hole ran a wooden paddle with a long handle and a disk on one end to splash the cream up and down until it turned into butter. Then there was a wooden butter mold with a woodcut top; when pressed on the butter it made a beautiful design. Also, there were waffle irons made specially for wood stoves that flipped over so they could brown on both sides, and wafer irons with long handles, generations old. A very interesting device was a peach peeler made of iron. A large adjustable screw clamped it to the edge of a table. When one turned the crank, the peeler part came in contact with the peach that was held securely on three prongs. So the interesting antiques were packed in a box and left in the pantry to be carried later to our new home. (That was the last time I ever saw my prize box. It mysteriously disappeared.)

Like a thief fleeing from captors, Time seemed to escape from us. The first of February scurried in before we realized it. Usually, it was a hard month on one's health—a good one for pneumonia. The weather was either very cold and rainy or very cold and windy. But that year Nature's understanding spirit cooperated with the Ellenton people 100 per cent. She'd already contributed warm fall days soaked in sunshine, followed by a mild winter with little rain. And, as we approached the spring months, it was amazing how Nature continued to exert her benign power to help ease the burden of the changeover: She not only sensed our practical needs of a balmy spring but also gratified our aesthetic feelings by giving us an early blooming season. Masses of spring flowers added beauty to the garden, and the white dogwood tree near the kitchen was lovelier than ever before. Nature's kindness even astounded house-movers and contractors. They agreed that they couldn't have had better weather for moving and building houses. Otherwise, the evacuation couldn't have gone along so smoothly. I still think about it in amazement.

Above all else, the people were thankful no one had been seriously ill or died during those frantic fifteen months. In fact, the people seemed unusually healthy. It was hard to believe a statement that Dr. Paul Culbreath, our family physician, made to me: "Only a tenth of the people will survive this ordeal of transplantation." But his prediction came true: One death after another occurred in the next two years and Dr. Culbreath was among them.

One afternoon as I drove my car into the garage, I saw Mamie's already there. I hurried in to see why she'd come home earlier than usual. She was sitting at the dining room table making out a list. "You didn't go to Aiken this morning?" I asked, as I flopped into a chair opposite hers.

She put her pencil down and looked at me. "No. I decided I needed you to go with me to Augusta this afternoon to select tile for the bathrooms." She hesitated a moment and continued, "It's well I *was* here this morning."

"Why?" I asked, startled.

"Would you believe it, Another appraiser came!"

"Another! Why the entire house is in disorder; it looks like a whirlwind has passed through it."

I was thinking about the cardboard boxes scattered over the house that were filled with heterogeneous heaps of trash destined for the bonfire; and the dust that had accumulated on the floors and furniture over several weeks. Then, too, the rugs had been piled one upon another in the living room, waiting for the cleaners to pick them up. The house couldn't have been more topsy-turvy.

"Goodness," I exclaimed, shaking my head, "when *will* the Government make up its mind about our house?"

"That's the answer I'd like to have." Mamie picked up her pencil and unconsciously began making the figure eight on her list.

"Well," I said, rising from the table, "if the appraiser couldn't see the value of the house between boxes and dust, we're sunk."

"It certainly means the money for our home isn't even in sight." Mamie continued tracing her figure eight until it was now inky black.

"Give me a minute and we'll get going. Just try to forget the whole thing," I called back over my shoulder as I left the room. But I knew neither one of us would be able to do that.

Since the repeated appraisals of our home had covered many months, Mamie and I were surprised when an agent visited us about two weeks later with an offer from the Government. We had of course discussed the compensation we'd consider fair, but we were disappointed to find the offer was short of our figure by several thousand dollars.

The following afternoon we discussed it with a lawyer. He told us that if we sued, according to previous cases, we'd probably win an increase. But expenses of the suit would reduce our gain to practically nothing. All in all he said, it was best to negotiate with the Government on the base of its offer. Reluctantly, we followed the lawyer's advice.

By now it was evident that our house in Aiken wouldn't be ready for occupancy in March. In fact we'd do well to move in by April. So about ten days before evacuation day, Mamie and I notified a Government official we'd have to stay in Ellenton beyond the deadline.

Nonchalantly, he replied, "Lock up your house just as it is, and get a boarding place."

This heartless suggestion incensed us. "*No*," I said, looking him straight in the eyes. "We're *not* leaving Ellenton until we take our furniture."

So indignant was Mamie, there was hardly the pause of a comma between my angry reply to the official and hers. Pointing her forefinger at him, she began preaching: "*You know as well as we do, there'd be nothing left in the house or on the premises by April. We're not leaving.*"

She and I knew only too well what was happening to vacated buildings—even doorknobs, hinges and the like were disappearing. So it didn't matter how rough life got, we were determined to stick it out.

Chapter VII

IN MY HEART FOREVER

It was hardly dawn—just light enough for objects in the room to capture an outline appearance. But I was glad to wake up; it had been a night of fitful sleeping and confused dreaming. Desperately I squirmed free from the tangled bedclothes that bound my body, making me look like an Egyptian mummy. One pillow had absented itself from the bed; and, with a few more of my contortions, the other would've soon followed. I retrieved the pillows, restored the covering in place, and lay back; it was too soon to get up.

Immediately my mind began acting like a pendulum, swinging back and forth from the present to the past and vice versa. Today, Sunday, February 24, 1952, the Baptist Church—older than Ellenton itself—would conclude a ministry that had continued uninterrupted for one hundred forty-seven years. My knowledge of its historical struggle to exist and grow made me doubly sad that its doors would now have to close forever.

On October 13, 1805, the Union Church of Christ, located on the Upper Runs, started life with thirty members. Thirty-four years later in 1839, it suffered almost complete extinction: Alexander Campbell, United States religious leader and founder of the church called Disciples of Christ or Christian Church (nicknamed "Campbellites"), came over from Augusta, Georgia, into South Carolina to preach. The majority of members in the Union Church followed his teachings and claimed the building. This was the birth of the Christian Church in the community.

At once the few remaining Baptists began to reorganize. Until they could build a church, they used an old Indian cave near Runs Bridge (later called Double Bridges) for a place of

DEDICATION SERVICES

OF THE

ELLENTON BAPTIST CHURCH

ELLENTON, S. C.

1805

Dedicated March 19, 1893
Burned August 8, 1922

1923

Dedicated April 1, 1923

APRIL FIRST TO FIFTH
NINETEEN HUNDRED AND TWENTY-THREE

[72]

Home Coming Services

July 29, 1951

The Ellenton Baptist Church

Ellenton, South Carolina

1805 - 1951

The altar and choir loft in the Ellenton Baptist Church.

worship. Minutes from their first conferences stated: They felt
that as a body the Union Church of Christ, given that name for
the sake of peace and harmony, had intruded upon and interrupted their rights. To avoid strife, they would no longer worship
in the old house. They now proposed building a regular orthodox
Baptist Church subject alone to its government. In a short time
the finance committee had raised $1010. Another committee had
selected a site near the Runs Bridge for the new church; and
the small congregation had called a pastor.

Fifty-four years later on March 19, 1893, the Baptist Church
had grown sufficiently to build and dedicate a beautiful sanctuary
in the young town of Ellenton. After twenty-nine years of service, on August 8, 1922, lightning struck and burned the building;
only the furnishings were saved. In less than a year on April 1,
1923, another church with a sanctuary and an educational building stood in its place. After twenty-eight years of progress it
would close its doors today at noon. The Church would pass into
history.

Mostly members would participate in this final service; those
who had recently moved would return, if possible, for this
poignant occasion. Previously, on July 29, 1951, the Church had
observed Homecoming Day. Former pastors as far back as 1921,
and out-of-town members had crowded into the sanctuary to bid
farewell to the institution that had served as a mighty impetus
in molding their lives. Between the morning and afternoon
services, the Church had entertained with one of Ellenton's
famous barbecues. Although the day had been tinged with sad-
ness, there was a note of joy in the reunion. But today would be
different: No one would find happiness in the last service; it
would be more like attending the last rite of a close friend.

Concerned over an incident that had occurred after church
service almost a year ago, I guarded my optimism over our final
service ending peacefully. I could only hope it would. Photographers, true to their profession, had persisted in trying to attend

a worship service to take pictures. Such a performance would've really upset the congregation. Besides, the Church loathed publicity; only those who had come to worship were welcome. I suspected, as everyone else had, too, that eventually photographers would waylay the congregation leaving church. This right was theirs, but a right that would prove dangerous; for the people were weary of such. Their nerves were as threadbare as the clothing of the shabbiest tramp. They could take no more without strong reactions against any offender. Realizing the touchy situation, several members warned the photographers of the consequences; but they didn't heed the advice.

One Sunday morning after services had begun, I noticed from the choir loft (I played the organ facing the congregation) several members, all men, coming in late and slipping quietly into the back pew. Nearly always those who attended regularly sat just about in the same place from Sunday to Sunday. From observation I'd learned the favorite pew of each family; so, with a sweep of my eyes over the congregation, I realized these men weren't in their regular places. *That alerted me. Was something brewing?* I'd reason: they'd come in late; naturally they sat on the back seat. Apparently nothing was wrong. Nervously, I watched them; for somehow I didn't have confidence in my reasoning that morning.

During the singing of the last song, I lost contact with the men. But while Mr. Parkinson was pronouncing the benediction, standing by the foyer door as he always did to speak to everyone afterward, I had the opportunity to peep over the heads of the standing congregation. When I saw those men heading for the foyer, passing stealthily by Mr. Parkinson like an animal sneaking by its enemy, *I knew something was about to happen.*

I felt sure no one was aware of any turmoil outside: The people didn't hurry, and after they'd gone, Mr. Parkinson returned to his study. But when I'd played the last chord of the postlude, I scurried from the loft like a scared mouse. Running down the aisle of the empty church, I burst through the swinging doors into the foyer and snatched open the front door. There was plenty to see:

A free-for-all fight had taken place. The Ellenton men had finished their job in seconds and quietly vanished from the scene. Bruised photographers emerged from the melee with bloody noses, torn coats and shirts. Broken cameras were strewn in every direction. The owners were still gathering up the pieces when I jumped into my car and hurried away. The incident was regrettable, but I couldn't help feeling that the stubborn photographers had brought it on themselves.

My reminiscing ended abruptly. When the grandfather clock in the downstairs hall struck eight, I bounced out of bed and dressed hurriedly.

The weather was warmer than normal for late February. It wasn't raining—for which I was thankful—but the Clouds looked unfriendly. It would be tragic if they hid the sunshine on a day when we desperately needed it to make the world look less gloomy. Before I left for church I thought the Clouds had reconsidered. But no-o-o. They allowed the Sun to peek in and out among them for a short time, then caged him in securely. Anyhow the gray day was in keeping with the spirits of the people.

A little before 11 o'clock I sat calmly at the organ waiting for those last few minutes to elapse before starting. A solemn congregation waited, too. The silence that permeated the sanctuary was almost eerie. Occasionally, a stifled cough or an opening door interrupted the hush. My eyes roamed over the congregation. No one there could veil his feelings. For many, suffering had etched itself deeply into their faces. There were no tears to relieve their emotions—they'd dried up long ago. Others were still battling their feelings. By pressing their lips tightly together, they'd hardened the lines around their mouths.

I'd steeled myself to participate in this final service by pretending it was just an ordinary Sunday. But my depressed spirits refused to go along with my pretense. My fingers moved automatically over the keys producing mechanical sounds and my leaden feet dragged the peddle board. My entire body felt heavy. I was trembling inwardly when I slid off the bench into the chair by the organ to listen to the sermon.

In a deliberate manner Mr. Parkinson took his place behind the lectern. He looked with deep concern at his familiar congregation; then suddenly, he realized he couldn't continue. In a broken voice, he said, "I cannot preach." And sat down.

The Board of Deacons then came forward. The chairman called the roll and presented the members with letters, attesting their membership, which they'd need to transfer to other churches.

After the benediction I played the postlude softly as the people filed by Mr. Parkinson at the front door to say goodby to a beloved pastor who had refused to leave his people until the end.

The next day an intense desire swept over me to see the church intact once more. So I returned alone to engrave on my mind and heart everlasting memories of its physical aspect and to feel again its spiritual impact.

The straight cement walk on which I stood led to the portico, the front entrance into the church. Its slender double columns on either side of the front supported an unadorned entablature and pediment. Directly above the portico was a round white-wooden frame enclosing a stained glass design. The portico also centered the facade of the church that featured formal balance. Flanked on either side were standard-size rectangular memorial windows with medallion designs in multicolored dark hues. In the rear to the left of the sanctuary was the educational building. It, too, featured windows similar to those on the front.

I realized this small, neat, gray-stucco building wouldn't look very imposing to outsiders, but to me, it had never looked so appealing as it nestled peacefully within its foundation shrubbery. I couldn't imagine anyone disturbing it.

Like an automaton, I walked toward the portico. As I passed the bare spot where the outdoor bulletin board had stood only yesterday, I closed my eyes tightly and shuddered. From the portico, I entered the narrow foyer through outside double doors with an archlike span of stained glass over them. Pushing open the varnished inside swinging doors that separated the foyer and sanctuary, I stood within while my eyes made a panorama of the sanctuary.

The late afternoon February sun shined weakly through the memorial windows on the west side, giving the sanctuary an air of awe. The inscription, "In Memory of . . ." on each window brought blinding tears. Quickly I wiped them away. As I moved on I was impressed with the beauty of the mahogany pews extending between the two outside red-carpeted aisles. Reaching the front pew, I sat down.

To my right was the baby grand piano. The very sight of it evoked such memories as to quicken my heart beat. Deliberately, I turned my head. Centered below the pulpit was the marble-top communion table with plain straight-back chairs on either side. My eyes traveled up to the pulpit. Behind the solid, heavy lectern on which the massive old Bible rested was a high-back antique chair carved at the top like the letter "W" with the center point higher. The back was wood except for the middle which, like the seat, was overstuffed with red velvet. Two similar, but smaller chairs were on either side.

Behind the pulpit was the elevated, recessed choir loft. On the left was the entrance door for the choir to center. Between the wall and chancel rail was a narrow passageway on either side, used as an entrance to and from the pulpit. Chimes hung on the back wall between two small memorial windows comparable in colors to the larger ones in the sanctuary. Below the chimes was the organ, the organ I loved so much. . . .

No longer could I sit there! No longer was I an automaton! Up the pulpit steps I leaped, then on into the choir loft! Sliding onto the bench, I quickly opened the organ, turned on the switch, and began playing with a joyful heart. But, my ecstasy was soon over. Numbly, I closed the organ and walked slowly out of the church. Then quietly, I closed the door as though in the presence of death. *But somehow I knew the memories of that visit would live in my heart forever.*

Chapter VIII

OUR LAST WEEK

It was the last week of Ellenton's life. Never had the town experienced such activity. It was paradoxical: House-movers, working overtime, lined highways; trailer residents, scattered over the community for the past year, rolled out leaving bare spots surrounded by dead leaves with a foot path leading to where the trailer door once was; freight trains continually bringing in more and more equipment caused traffic jams around the depot; commuters employed at the plant congested traffic in early morning and late afternoon.

The school also experienced excessive activity: Teachers struggled to pack and label boxes containing contents of their classrooms, including text books, to meet the deadline by noon Friday so the government could move them to the new school in Jackson. And to add to that frantic pace, the graduating class, as a sentimental remembrance, worked feverishly to present their class play (a highlight of their senior year) in the Ellenton school auditorium.

Neither was there a lull in the post office nor in the telephone system: To get a long distance circuit was an accomplishment. From experience, I'd learned never to quit dialing. If my forefinger and patience lasted, sometime within an hour I'd be lucky and grab the line.

Even though moving by March 1 was impossible, enough problems had spilled over into the last week to make it one of the busiest yet, and each problem needed immediate attention. One of the knottiest posers was transferring a set of chimes from the Ellenton Church to the First Baptist Church in Aiken. Our family had presented these chimes in memory of our parents.

[81]

The Ellenton Church had returned them to us so they could continue as a memorial. At a brief service in the First Baptist Church in Aiken one Sunday morning in February, Mr. Parkinson presented them on behalf of the family. I wanted the manufacturer of the chimes, located in Atlanta, Georgia, to move them, but I'd had no response from them to several urgent letters. It was like a miracle when I received a visit from a young friend, Marg McGraw, who lived in Atlanta. Previously, she'd taught school in Ellenton.

"You're an angel dropped down from heaven," I cried, hugging her.

"Not exactly," she said, laughing. Then in a concerned tone, "You've needed me for something?"

"Definitely. I've a problem that only you can help me solve."

"Only me?" She looked as if it were hard to believe.

Marg listened intently to my plight. "You understand," I said, "if the chimes aren't moved this week, the manufacturer may have trouble getting into Ellenton. *Please*, get someone here immediately."

Marg squeezed my hand. *"I'll get them here on time."*

Two days later the chimes were on their way to Aiken.

In the midst of such a hectic life, a rumor had persisted all week that the Government would cut off the town's electricity at midnight on February 29. If the report were true, families left in Ellenton would have a sampling of primitive living. In our home electricity ran everything except the heating system. However, by stocking the pantry with groceries that needed no cooking, we could manage about meals. Without too much inconvenience, candles, flashlights, and longer days could tide us over without lights. *But without water life would be hard.*

Exactly how long we'd have to live under such circumstances, there was no way of knowing at the time. So to meet the situation—should it happen—Mamie and I worked all afternoon filling bathtubs, pots, pans, and every available container we could find with water. As a last resort, we could use water from a flowing artesion well near the depot. But I didn't feel comfortable over the thought of such a life.

"Do you think the Government would deprive us of electricity to retaliate for not leaving on time?" I asked Mamie as she came into the kitchen with more containers she'd found in the yard.

"The Government should realize we preferred leaving when others did. We've been caught in a predicament not of our choosing," Mamie said, as she filled the jars she'd just brought in.

I continued watching her, but my mind was reaching back into my childhood to a windy day when I flew a kite. The kite soared so fast that the wind tugged the string from my hands. I stood watching it ascend on its zig-zag way until it merged with the grayness of the sky. Like the kite, the sleepy little town of Ellenton was fast disappearing into the shadows of approaching death. I could hold her no longer. The time had come for parting; I wanted to leave. It was punishment to stay.

The night was unusually warm and still for February. Restless and knowing sleep was far from me, I slipped down stairs to the front porch where I could walk and watch. Except for the street lights, which gave me a sense of protection, and an occasional patrol car passing, I was completely alone. Without knowing why, I walked slowly to the road. I could see the headlights of cars coming from the direction of the school house and turning toward the highway. By that, I knew the senior play was over. For a few moments the natural scene gave me a fleeting feeling of normalcy.

I was too fidgety to linger long. Habit took me straight to the three-seated green swing that hung from the ceiling of the porch by iron chains. Resting my left arm on the arm of the swing and using my right foot in a toe-heel rhythm like the motion of a rocking chair, I could co-ordinate the movement of the swing with my foot. Then I felt calmer—at least for half an hour.

Suddenly, I braced my foot against the floor and stopped dead still. I saw the western sky light up. I listened intently for thunder but none followed. "Sheet lightning," I said, and started the swing back into motion. But the sky persisted in brightening up; and now I was sure I heard thunder. I wasn't surprised by the approaching thunder storm. We'd often had them in winter months when unseasonable warm weather existed. So I continued sitting in the swing, listening to the crescendo of the thunder as if it were music. But when bolts of lightning began zigzagging across the sky, revealing inky clouds, I left the swing and stood at the head of the steps to get a better view. Suddenly, a car dashed into our porte-cochere, and a middle-aged man jumped out. He ran up the porch steps; I quickly moved back to the front door and stepped inside. Before I could say a word he asked excitedly, "Are you in trouble?"

"No-o-o," I replied half scared and half embarassed. "How did you know I was out here?"

"By the flash of lightning. If you need me I'll be glad to help you. I'm a patrolman with du Pont."

Mamie heard us talking and came downstairs as fast as one of those flashes of lightning. "What's wrong?" she asked, looking quickly from one to the other. Her usual soft voice was now high and full of anxiety.

I explained the situation and the patrolman's presence.

"I didn't know you were on the porch or I would've joined you," she said, looking at me.

"Have you heard that the Government is going to cut off the town's electricity at midnight?" I asked the patrolman in a troubled voice.

"No, I haven't heard that. But if it's true, and you need my assistance, I'll gladly give it."

His offer seemed genuine, and it was good to know someone was close around to call on.

After the patrolman had left, Mamie stayed on. Like me she couldn't sleep. So we kept our vigil together, sometimes walking, sometimes sitting in silence; for the rain had begun falling and it was hard to talk above it. Then, as though Thor himself had taken over, one peal of thunder after another followed the vivid lightning, which was cutting the sky like a sword.

"Let's go inside," I shouted; for by now I was thoroughly frightened.

"You're just as safe here as anywhere," Mamie said calmly, and pushed her chair to a new position where she could get a better view of the storm's display. She actually seemed to enjoy it.

I knew I couldn't convince her otherwise. Like our father, she wasn't afraid of anything. But I couldn't sit still any longer. I began my lone march back and forth across the porch, stopping only when the lightning revealed the angry black sky and the deafening thunder roared like a tornado. Then I'd shut my eyes tight and clasp my hands over my ears.

The rain was now coming down in sheets, making the street lights look like blobs of yellow paint. "Even the elements resent Ellenton's death," I exclaimed above the thunderous din of the storm as I passed Mamie on my march.

"Evidently, they do," she shouted back.

It must have been at least twenty minutes—an eternity to me—before the rain slackened and the lightning and thunder became less intense.

"I think that downpour was the grand finale," Mamie said, rising from her chair.

"Let's hope so," I said, with a sigh of relief. "I didn't enjoy the show as much as you did."

The street lights had come into view again, and Mamie seemed satisfied to go inside. Just as we entered the front door, the hall clock began striking. We stopped to count: "One . . . two . . . three . . . four . . . five . . ." On the twelfth stroke, a terrific flash of lightning turned darkness into day. Out went the lights! We knew the answer now.

Without lighting candles, Mamie and I felt our way upstairs. The constant battle to meet the problems of the long, weary day and the frightening experience of the storm had sapped my strength and enervated my spirits. I fell into bed and knew nothing until hours later when I was startled by an electric light flashing on in my room.

Days later, we heard that a judge had ordered the Government to turn on the electricity and keep it on as long as anyone remained in Ellenton. Or, who knows? Perhaps it was only a quirk of nature that had coincided with the supposed threat.

Chapter IX

A STRANGER IN MY OWN HOME

Next morning, Saturday, March 1, our telephones were taken out. Left with no communication of any kind, we were living in complete isolation as prisoners in our own home. Except for a few buildings the Government had reserved temporarily for offices, the town was empty. There were no stores, no service stations, no doctors, no ambulance service, no anything except a horde of hungry cats and dogs and three human families.

Unfortunately, the garden no longer gave Mamie and me any pleasure. Neglected for lack of labor, it was fast returning to a state of nature. So even though bright sunshine flooded the deceased town after the terrific thunderstorm of the night before and the temperature had dropped sufficiently to promise a cool, pleasant day outdoors, both of us preferred to remain inside.

Furthermore, the death of Ellenton had grieved me as much as if the town had been a close friend. From past experiences I knew the tension I'd always lived under from the hour a loved one died until the last rites were over. Only then, resignation and adjustment would set in. Today I'd reached that point. The last rites were over and it suited me to lounge the week-end away.

Early Monday morning before plant commuters congested traffic, I was on my way to our new school in Jackson. This would be my introduction to it. No doubt, I thought, the novelty of the new building and the strange surroundings would distract teachers and pupils for a few days. Otherwise, the transition should be smooth since every item had been packed carefully and all boxes labeled.

As I turned into the untidy school grounds, still littered with pieces of castoff building materials, a modern wooden structure loomed up before me. Carefully, I meandered around the debris and made my way into the entrance hall. For a moment my throat tightened with the nostalgic thought of the traditional brick schoolhouse left behind. I heard angry voices in the distance and walked toward them. Like a mannequin I stood motionless as I stared upon a shocking scene—disgusted and indignant teachers diving into what looked like a pile of rubbish to recover their children's textbooks and other items belonging to their rooms. Instead of stacking boxes, the movers had dumped them in a heap in the middle of the floor. For days it was like digging out after a disaster to find what belonged where.

The mental and physical exertion of that day stripped us teachers of our last reserve of strength and patience. When I got home that afternoon, I flopped on Mamie's nap-taking sofa and fell into an exhausted sleep. Not until the doorbell had rung several times was I conscious enough to get up. Then in confusion I staggered toward the telephone, reaching for the receiver only to remember it was gone. It had to be the doorbell. I was still groggy when I opened the front door.

"You were asleep; and I've waked you up." Mildred, my cousin from Augusta, looked regretfully at me.

"No apologies necessary; it's wonderful to see you."

"Mamma is in the car. She longs to see Ellenton once more. I wasn't sure I'd get in, but no one stopped me. Can you go with us?" As Mildred spoke her big blue eyes swam with tears.

"Of course. I'm afraid though she won't be happy over what she sees," I said, as I hastened to get my coat and bag.

On our sad tour we stopped by the Baptist Church; but every entrance into the sanctuary and the educational building was locked. So Mildred and I crossed over to the house next door and sat on the floor of the porch with our legs dangling over the side. Aunt Addie continued to walk around. Finding a door unlocked at the back of the church, she opened it and stepped into the furnace room. Not expecting a step down, she fell. Her screams brought us running.

Aunt Addie's large, stout body was crumpled on the cement floor like a limp piece of cloth. In a sitting position with her back to the door, and holding her head down in her hands, she kept repeating between sobs and moans, "My feet . . . my feet . . ."

Mildred's first impulse was to get into the little furnace room with her. "No, don't!" I cried, barring her with my arm. "There's not enough room. We can work better from the outside."

I pushed the door wide open. Mildred and I straddled the doorsill and each linked her arms under one of Aunt Addie's. Slowly, we dragged her to the door and carefully lifted her to a sitting position on the doorsill before we stretched her out on the hard ground.

"I *must* get help. Can you manage without me?" I asked, as I looked at Aunt Addie's feet turned limply to the side. I could see both were broken.

"Yes, but *please* hurry and get something to ease her pain."

Aunt Addie's moans had grown louder; her pleading eyes sent me running toward the car. Just as I ran around the corner of the church, a patrolman drove up. "Are you in trouble?" he called after me.

"Yes. Go to the back of the church!" I pointed the direction but kept on running. I fumbled until I finally started the car and drove off as if I were the patrolman running down a law-breaker.

"A pain killer . . . a pain killer . . ." I kept repeating. The only pain killers I had at home were some pills the doctor had given me several years ago for abdominal cramps brought on by nervous tension.

I returned with these pills, some water, and a pillow. The patrolman and Mildred had moved Aunt Addie to the front lawn and she was chewing aspirin he had given her. I wondered why I hadn't thought of aspirin. Knowing an ambulance was necessary, I had the patrolman call Jackson for the same one that had formerly served Ellenton. In minutes Aunt Addie and Mildred were on their way to the University Hospital in Augusta.

After writing Mamie a hasty note, I followed in Mildred's car and stayed at the hospital until matters were in hand. It was eleven o'clock that night when I finally got home.

The hectic day had left me extremely tired and edgy. Sleep was far away, so I passed the hours reliving those out-of-the-ordinary events and worrying about my unfitness for next day's work. But one consoling thought kept passing through my mind —patrolmen were always there whenever any emergency arose. I was thankful for them.

Some time during the early morning hours, the wheels in my head ceased turning, and I lost consciousness. It seemed only a few minutes between then and the time the alarm clock rang. The ringing irritated me; I was still tired and not ready to get up. I grabbed the clock, pushed in the alarm, and set it down impatiently on the bedside table. "Now you'll hush." To my complete amazement my words came out in a whisper. I was dumfounded. Quickly, I sat up in bed; now I was wide awake. "What's wrong with my voice?" This question came in a whisper, too.

I had no way to communicate with the school, so I'd have to ride to Jackson and explain my absence. Throwing on my robe, I went across the hall to Mamie's room. She was already up. "I've lost my voice," I whispered, putting my hand to my throat.

"You've what?" Mamie said, stopping her dressing and looking astonished.

"I've lost my voice," I whispered as loudly as I could.

"Dress to go to Augusta; I'm taking you to a doctor." Mamie began to hurry as though it were an emergency. Certainly I couldn't teach without a voice, so I was willing to go. On the way we'd stop by the school and tell the superintendent.

The doctor's diagnosis was that strain and tension had brought on laryngitis. Pent up emotions, he said, could play all kinds of tricks on the human body. That day I resolved to give expression to my feelings more than I'd done in the past. Surprisingly, the opportunity came sooner than I'd expected: Several days later I tripped over rugs the cleaners had brought back the previous week and sprained my ankle. I did what was natural: I cried. "What else . . . is going . . . to happen to me?" I sobbed in a squeaky, hoarse voice.

Mamie became alarmed, "*Are you hurt that bad?*"

I shook my head vehemently.

"Then why are you crying? You've never acted this way."

"I'm not repressing . . . my emotions any more," I said in a hysterical voice.

"Well go ahead if that's it." Mamie seemed relieved as she hurried off to prepare the hot and cold water treatment used for sprained ankles.

By the end of two weeks I was living a tripartite life again—home at night, in Jackson during school hours, and in Aiken or Augusta every afternoon. However, my sick leave had been a lifesaver. Sleeping late every morning and not living on a schedule, refreshed my frayed nervous system like rain refreshes the parched earth. During that time Mamie and I spent many absorbing hours in consultation with a decorator. We were soon to see the home we'd dreamed of so long materialize into reality.

But by no means had we solved all our problems. They kept popping up like noxious weeds in a flower garden. Some were disheartening, some aggravating, some actually humorous.

I can always laugh about the afternoon Mamie and I returned from Aiken with several large bags of groceries, including a juicy steak for our supper. Mamie waited on the backporch steps until I could unlock the kitchen door. Before we got the first bag in, a three-legged dog and several cats wild from hunger pounced upon the groceries. I ran out to help Mamie fight them off. We managed to salvage everything but the steak—the three-legged dog got it for his supper. Then we knocked cats every direction and ran in with the bags.

"We've *got* to get rid of all those stray cats and that three-legged dog," Mamie said at supper that night.

"I'll bring some cotton sacks to catch the cats in. When you get out of the area you can turn 'em out." Arthur told us.

But the problem wasn't solved that easily. Coaxing wild cats into a sack—even a baited sack—proved to be impossible. Finally one did go in. We quickly tied him up, put him in the car, and drove to a place were we could release him. But en route he cut such capers, I became as scared as the cat. He would jump as high as the sack permitted, and that was almost over the front seat. It took both Mamie and me to untie the sack to let the cat out. I look upon it now as a heroic act—one I don't care to repeat. Right there I made a decision and Mamie agreed: Those cats could remain in the ghost town of Ellenton.

One problem that exasperated us was a Government agent continually coming at night to inquire when we'd vacate the house. At first, I'd inform him of the progress of our house in Aiken so he'd understand how much longer we'd have to stay. But when his visits became more and more frequent, I began to say, "I don't know."

One night as I was making sandwiches for supper, the doorbell rang. "I know it's that Government man, Mr. Bell, tormenting us again," I said to Mamie, as I wheeled around to answer the ring.

"You're not going to the door with the knife, I hope." Mamie looked at me in surprise.

I looked at the knife in my hand and grinned. "Yes, I think I will."

"Good evening," Mr. Bell said in a pleasant manner, then backed away a little when he eyed my knife.

"Good evening," I replied with no intonation in my voice.

An awkward silence followed. Then, "Er . . ."

"Yes, I understand. When are we moving?" I let my voice register irritation.

"Well . . . er . . . you know this property belong to the Government," he finally blurted out.

"It does not belong to the Government." I was indignant. *"We haven't received one penny of money for it."*

Mr. Bell not only kept his eye on the knife but also kept his distance. Then he flung words at me that hurt as much as though he'd stabbed me with the knife. "This house became the property of the Government on January 21, 1952."

Was he saying the house I was born in and had lived in all my life wasn't mine? For a moment I stared beyond him into the darkness. I shivered inwardly at the thought; then dizziness overwhelmed me. I steadied myself by grasping the open door with my free hand and clutching the knife tightly in my other. I am a stranger in my own home, I thought.

Mr. Bell sensed my emotional struggle. His words brought me back to reality. "I'm sorry."

I disregarded his sympathy and asked, "Who owns the street in front of this house?"

"The Government."

"Well *please* tell the Government if it needs this house so badly, it can move us into the street; for our house in Aiken isn't ready for occupancy."

That was his last visit. But next day I noticed a large sign stretched across a row of bannisters on our front porch: THIS IS GOVERNMENT PROPERTY.

The problem that was most disheartening was Mamie and I hadn't yet received a check from the Government for our seized property. Several weeks had elapsed since we'd signed to accept the inadequate offer. We decided to see the Assistant U. S. Attorney who had opened an office in Aiken to handle the take over of the plant site.

On a March day that had promised sunshine, we set out for Aiken as soon as I'd finished my day at school. On our way the weather reneged on us. A stiff, cold wind from the north pushed the sun behind dust clouds, and as if in glee over its achievement picked up grains of sand scattering them like feathers from one place to another.

Without doubt, people react to weather conditions: Just as warmth and sunshine bring composure and calmness, a cold, blustery day can make one edgy.

When we got to Aiken, I dropped Mamie at our new house and went on to talk with the Assistant Attorney. While I was waiting a woman stalked out of his office not bothering to close the door or even glance my way. With a grim look on her face, she rushed through the swinging doors in the corridor so fast that they oscillated at full speed. I hesitated to knock. Peering through the opened door, I saw a stern-faced man with slightly disheveled gray hair, sitting midway at a long oblong table covered with papers. One thin hand moved to and fro over his forehead as if he were rubbing a headache away. The other held a paper which he was studying. An untouched cup of coffee sat at his right elbow. It had grown cold during his raging battle of words with the woman who'd just stormed out.

Under these unfavorable conditions, I rapped lightly on the door; I was determined to keep my temper even if he should lose his. "Come in," a gruff voice said, without looking up. I walked to the empty chair across from him and stopped. "Sit down," he commanded in the same gruff voice. Then he looked up. I could feel his steel-like eyes piercing me. "What do you want to see me about?" There was no inflection in his voice.

I introduced myself, acquainted him with the facts about our home, and asked, "When will the Government pay us? We need the money badly."

That question triggered his anger. The tirade began: "You've delayed your own pay running to your lawyer to bring suit against the Government. Go back and pay him to draw up the condemnation papers." (The Government had to condemn entailed property before possessing it.)

"But . . ." I stammered, holding my temper, "the Government . . . is supposed to do that."

"*The Government isn't going to do it!*" he shouted. Then, beating his chest with his fist, he exclaimed, "*I want you to know, I am the Government.*"

I could feel hot blood rushing to my head and I knew my eyes were flashing with anger. Beating *my chest* with *my fist*, I retorted, "*Yes, and I want to remind you that I am 'we the people.'*"

With that, I stormed out exactly like the woman before me. When I stopped for Mamie, one look told her what had happened. "Move over, let me drive," she said. "Now, let it out your system. What did the Old Goat say?"

Next day I was too upset to teach. So Mamie and I went back to Aiken to discuss our situation with another Government official who we hoped might help us. The wind had blown itself out and allowed the sun to shine. There was the promise of a warm day. The weather was as propitious to our purpose as it had been unfavorable the day before. Relatively few people were there that morning, so we were ushered in immediately to talk with the other official. There was no reason I can think of why the door was left ajar, but if it hadn't been, our check from the Government might have been delayed for several more months.

The attorney with whom I'd tried to talk with the previous afternoon passed by the open door and recognized me. He came in. His presence disconcerted me for a moment; but I soon noticed his stern face of yesterday had dissolved into a soft, genteel expression. His eyes were apologetic, and his frail physique gave the impression of being overworked. But, with his hair brushed back showing his forehead, he looked every inch a gentleman.

"I want to apologize for my rudeness yesterday," he said. "It was one of those exasperating days, but I shouldn't have taken it out on you. I've come to offer my assistance."

Never in my life had I so completely disliked a person one day, only to admire him the next. I gladly accepted his apology, his explanation, and his offer of assistance. He subsequently proved himself a good friend and pushed our check through as fast as possible.

With light hearts we left the courthouse. And after talking with our contractor, we were exhilarated by his news that in a week we could occupy the house even though the kitchen wouldn't be finished until later. Compared to other problems we'd faced, Mamie and I were positive we could meet this one.

During the last week, our emotions were torn between the love of the old home and the anticipation of the new one waiting for us. Physically tired from packing that couldn't be done until the very last day, we had no trouble sleeping that last night. Next morning with stout determination, we supervised the loading of the van. After it had left, we walked out the front door, locked it, got into our separate cars, and followed the van to Aiken. Not once did we look back. A new life was ahead; we'd left the old.

Chapter X

CONCLUSION

Riding out of Ellenton on April 1, after living a month in a ghost town, was like riding from darkness into light. For fifteen months our patience had been sorely tried; mentally and physically we were weary. Often the many hurdles had seemed almost insurmountable, but time had taken care of them. And time would help everyone adjust to his adopted home and have happiness once more.

Looking back I realize, as many others do also, why the Savannah River Plant is necessary: International tension that developed when the Soviet Union successfully tested its first atomic weapon forced the United States to keep abreast in her defense program. Our Government needed special materials for nuclear weapons and it needed the Savannah River Plant to produce them.

I also understand why the Government in search of a site for the largest single construction job ever undertaken selected Ellenton and the surrounding areas out of 114 potential sites in all sections of the country. The reasons were justifiable:

Millions of gallons of water, low in mineral content, to remove great quantities of heat generated in the reactors was a must. The Savannah River answered that need perfectly.

Then the terrain and topography of this large land area of 200,831 acres or 315 square miles were conducive to rapid construction. It was also large enough to space manufacturing facilities at distances that would best serve the interest of security and safety. Another factor was that fewer people lived in this area compared with any other suitable site of comparable size. The Government paid $18,975,000 to move about 6,000 people

[97]

and 6,100 graves. Another area elsewhere would have cost even more.

Today, our little town of Ellenton is just a beautiful memory, one I'll keep forever; no human agent can take it from me. The sacrifice required was heartbreaking, but in no way is it comparable to the lives that have been given on battlefields for our Country. So we small town folk are proud to have played a part in helping to preserve and protect our United States of America.

Lightning Source UK Ltd.
Milton Keynes UK
UKOW02f1617080816

280214UK00003B/232/P